W9-APH-489

Table of Contents

A Baker's Dozen of
Lessons Learned
from the
Teaching Trenches

#1 Teacher

1. Teachers Make A Difference
2. Good Parenting Is Underrated
3. Passion Is Powerful
4. We Become Whom We Hang Out With
5. To Each His or Her Own
6. Reading Matters

Author
Danny Brassell, Ph.D.
Foreword by Will Hobbs

SHELL EDUCATION

MAY 1 1

Tualatin Public Library
18878 SW Martinazzi Avenue
Tualatin, OR 97062-7092
Member of Washington County Cooperative Library Services

A Baker's Dozen of Lessons Learned from the Teaching Trenches

Editor
Blane Conklin, Ph.D.

Assistant Editor
Leslie Huber, M.A.

Editorial Director
Lori Kamola, M.S.Ed.

Editor-in-Chief
Sharon Coan, M.S.Ed.

Editorial Manager
Gisela Lee, M.A.

**Creative Director/
Cover Design**
Lee Aucoin

Print Production Manager
Don Tran

Interior Layout Designer
Robin Erickson

Publisher
Corinne Burton, M.A.Ed.

Shell Education

5301 Oceanus Drive
Huntington Beach, CA 92649-1030

http://www.shelleducation.com

ISBN 978-1-4258-0520-3

© 2010 Shell Education

Made in U.S.A.

The names of teachers and students have been changed to protect their identities, except for the author's high school and college instructors.

The classroom teacher may reproduce copies of materials in this book for classroom use only. The reproduction of any part for an entire school or school system is strictly prohibited. No part of this publication may be transmitted, stored, or recorded in any form without written permission from the publisher.

Foreword

As you will learn in *A Baker's Dozen of Lessons Learned from the Teaching Trenches*, Danny Brassell was indeed a student of mine in my seventh-grade reading class in Durango, Colorado. What a pleasure it is for me to tell you a little about Danny and this gem of a book he has written.

About Danny . . . you'll find that he describes himself as "a bit of a handful" as a student. He was right about that, as was Wordsworth when he wrote, "the child is the father of the man." I would hasten to add that Danny was a handful in the very best way, a virtual Hadron Collider of positive energy, and so he remains today. After years in the teaching trenches in south central Los Angeles, he went on to become a teacher of teachers, the founder of the Lazy Readers' Book Club, and a speaker of national renown on the subjects of reading and education.

For the last number of years, I've been hearing tales of Danny from teachers who have attended his sessions. I finally got the chance myself, recently, at IRA's national reading conference in Phoenix. The house was packed, and he wowed 'em!

Here's the thing about Danny. You come away not only inspired, but with dozens of practical innovations to add to your own teaching bag of tricks. The man is a cornucopia of ideas and suggestions, and this book is not for teachers only. His chapter on parenting is a must-read for parents.

Do yourself a favor. Read this book. Try any chapter and you'll read the whole thing. It's laugh-out-loud funny and off-handedly, unpretentiously wise. His candor is refreshing; he doesn't pull punches. Negativity in all its guises is the enemy, and Danny's got no time for it.

Press your nose against Danny's classroom window. Those were lucky kids to have him as their teacher. Here's something Danny leaves us with as he nears the end of his book. It rang true for me as a longtime teacher, as it will ring true for you: "All that really matters is how you make your students feel through the things you say and do."

This book is a gift. Thank you, Danny.

Will Hobbs
author of popular children's books, including
the award-winning *Ghost Canoe*

Preface: Who Am I?

My name is Danny, and I am a teacher of students of all ages, cultures, shapes, and sizes. I have taught students ranging from preschoolers to rocket scientists. I can say that because I used to teach English as a second language to engineering students at the University of Southern California.

I became a teacher because of the movie *Stand and Deliver*. If you haven't seen it, do yourself a favor and rent a copy. It tells the inspirational true story of Jaime Escalante (played brilliantly by Edward James Olmos), who goes to Garfield High School in East Los Angeles to teach A.P. Calculus. I decided I was going to be just like Jaime Escalante, so I signed up to be a high school social studies teacher in the inner city. I spent the bulk of my teaching career working in Compton, California, located in south central Los Angeles. Along the way, I managed to work with high school students, middle school students, upper elementary school students, and very little children. However, instead of preparing students for college, I often found myself coming home with snot spots on the knees of my pants.

What I learned, more than anything, is that what works for a twelfth grader does not necessarily work for a kindergartner, but what works for a kindergartner works for all ages. Working with younger students helped me find my passion for teaching, and I began to understand that good teaching requires inspiration, perspiration, and motivation. This book is a compilation of the baker's dozen of lessons I've learned from the teaching trenches. I hope you enjoy it.

Danny Brassell, Ph.D.

To Eva Tolbert, who taught me how to handle the teaching trenches.

Acknowledgements

I am truly indebted to so many people, too numerous to name. I would like to highlight those who have spent the most time working on this book with me.

Shell Education is a lovely publisher. Tim Rasinski introduced me to Sharon Coan and Lori Kamola a couple of years ago. Since then, Lori has been a cheerleader who has encouraged me to write a lot more. Thanks for the push, Lori. Blane Conklin and Leslie Huber have been wonderful editors to work with on this particular book. Sometimes (well, most of the time) I need someone to tell me how to filter a joke in print, and Blane and Leslie have been very patient with me. The entire book could not happen without the support of Rachelle Cracchiolo and Corinne Burton. Thank you for your confidence in me.

I want to thank my friends who lent their names to the back cover. Diane Lapp, Doug Fisher, and Nancy Frey are wonderful colleagues from San Diego State University who have constantly provided me with support and encouragement. I revere their friendship and marvel at all they manage to do. Jim Grant has been a wonderful mentor in my speaking career. Last but not least, Laura Numeroff served on the Board of Directors for BookEnds, and I have always been amazed by Laura's generosity and sense of humor. She deserves all of her writing success.

Thank you, Will Hobbs, for encouraging my writing when I was an awkward seventh grader. All of Durango is proud of what you have accomplished as a writer, and I am grateful that you agreed to write the foreword to my book. You know how much I appreciate you and Jean.

My wife, Jeanie, is the most magnificent person I know. I love you, honey, and thank you for putting up with me. Thank you also to Kate, Sean, and baby Samantha. Whenever Daddy is on the road speaking, his heart and mind are with all of you. Nothing delights me more than reading aloud to all of you in bed at night.

Finally, I want to thank all the teachers, administrators, parents, and students I have been blessed to work with over the years. I have had the privilege to tour the country speaking to various groups, and I am continually inspired by what people in the teaching trenches have to endure every day. Teachers receive no medals and few accolades, but they truly guide our future. If it were up to me, there would be ticker-tape parades in your honor. I humbly bow to all of you.

Danny Brassell, Ph.D.

Inspiration

Good teaching begins with inspiration,
and inspiration comes from many places.

Chapter 1

Teachers Make a Difference

One variable supersedes all others in our schools. People can argue about the quality of school funding or any number of educational issues until they are blue in the face. But no amount of added funding, materials, or extra support can stand above this variable: teachers.

Teachers can have a negative impact.

First, you need to know something about me. I was a bit of a handful when I was a student. I spent many of my early years writing standards, washing chalkboards, and sitting in corners. One of my first teachers had my parents' phone number memorized. And it wasn't because they were good friends.

I didn't know any better. Let me give you some background on where my troubles began. From the time I was three years old, my grandfather (a good ole Irish cop from upstate New York) would sit me on his lap, drink a beer, and sing a song that he taught me. It went like this:

"Grandpa's Irish Drinking Song"

I like beer.
I like beer.
It makes me a jolly good
    fellow.
It helps me unwind,
And sometimes it makes me
    feel mellow.

Whiskey's too rough—
Champagne costs too much—
And vodka puts my mouth in
    gear.
So let me explain,
It's my little refrain:
As a matter of fact, I like beer.

My kindergarten teacher asked our class if any of us knew a song, and I promptly and proudly shot my hand into the air and proceeded to regale my classmates with Grandpa's Irish drinking song. Needless to say, I was not the teacher's pet ("pest" may have been a more appropriate moniker). It all went downhill from there.

By third grade, I had already attended a handful of different schools. Mrs. Almond was my third third-grade teacher. She hated my guts because I knew the proper capital of Maryland (Annapolis) and challenged her when she insisted it was Baltimore. She also hated a little song I used to sing in her class that mimicked a popular television commercial jingle at the time: "Almond Joy's got nuts!" I'd sing. This did not endear me to Mrs. Almond.

When I was in Mrs. Almond's class, I was perhaps the greatest artist ever to grace the corridors of Our Lady of Grace Elementary School. Classmates would ask me to color gorillas or draw tanks, and my drawings would earn widespread acclaim in the cafeteria.

One day, Mrs. Almond asked us all to draw a picture of a clown. I do not remember exactly what mine looked like, but I remember admiring my latest masterpiece and feeling the twinge of pride one feels when one has created something of true beauty. Nothing made me happier than drawing. Awe and inspiration truly surrounded my artistic excellence.

Mrs. Almond strolled around the classroom, commenting just loudly enough about each student's picture so that the entire class could hear her. When she hovered over me, I swelled with anticipation for the compliment she had for me. With an index finger on her lip, she frowned and commented, "Now, that's not too good, is it, Danny?"

Do you know what? That was the last day I drew a picture in school. Isn't it sad that one teacher's fleeting negative comment prompted me to give up my passion?

Mrs. Newcomb was the woman who turned me off from science. She was my ninth-grade life science teacher, and she never changed the tone of her voice. Compared to her, the old scratchy instructional science films seemed interesting. She could make statements with such a lack of inflection that my classmates and I debated whether she herself was a living creature. "Good morning, class," she'd utter in a tone normally reserved for radio static and dead air. Corpses have shown more life. It was as if she received her teacher certification from the Department of Motor Vehicles. She had the gift of making anything sound dull.

"Welcome to the wonderful and exciting world of science."

"The school is burning down."

"I have a large laceration above my left eyebrow. I am slowly bleeding to death as I speak."

Her class was torture. She could put me to sleep quicker than a bottle of cold medicine.

I can remember every bad habit, negative comment, and painful exercise that my worst teachers forced me to endure.

But I have also learned another thing: good teachers can have a tremendous impact. I was always blessed with terrific English teachers.

Mrs. Whitt was my eighth-grade English teacher. She was approximately 187 years old and four feet tall (in clogs). Her teeth reminded me of summer—some're here, and some're there. Her dresses highlighted the latest Puritan fashions, and her gray hair was tied so tightly in a bun that many of us speculated that it was responsible for her cantankerous demeanor.

I learned how to yawn without opening my mouth in Mrs. Whitt's class. She enforced a strict policy that no one was to yawn or slouch, or she'd whack that student with the meter stick she carried around. If a student protested and threatened to tell a parent or the principal, she'd cackle with delight like the Wicked Witch of the East and reply, "Who'd believe you? I'm a sweet little old lady." This woman terrified us.

Mrs. Whitt was "old school." She believed that the English language was to be memorized and diagrammed. She'd waddle around the room with a stopwatch around her neck, just waiting for the opportune moment to quiz students on some random grammatical point.

"Brassell," she'd yell with one hand on my shoulder and the other holding her stopwatch. "Tell me the six forms of the present tense of the verb *to be*. Go!"

I'd sit up and rapidly recite, "Present tense! I am! You are! He, she, it is. We are! You are! They are!" Mrs. Whitt would look at my time, shake her head, and say, "Not good." This woman was tough.

Her grading policy was simple. On any paper, one spelling mistake automatically earned a student a C, and two spelling mistakes resulted in an F. One grammatical mistake dropped a student to a C, and two grammatical mistakes dropped a student to an F. Keep in mind that this was before she even graded the content of the paper. Failure was not an option with Mrs. Whitt. She'd keep you in detention until midnight every day until you got something right. Even the football coach was terrified of this woman.

She had a tradition. Every year, she gave her top student a coveted penny. It was just a penny, and yet, we all wanted it. Out of 325 eighth graders, I took second place with a 98.7 percent. Gena Haskins had a 99.2 percent, but she was a nerd. Mrs. Whitt looked at my grade, frowned at me, and said, "Never settle for second best."

This woman freaked me out. But I'll tell you what: I am forever grateful to her because she taught me English. I learned grammar, and I learned how to spell, all thanks to Mrs. Whitt.

Without Mrs. Whitt, I could never have passed Ms. McClain's class. Ms. McClain was my eleventh-grade English teacher. She had been teaching for nearly 25 years, and in all her time as a teacher, the highest grade a student had ever received on Ms. McClain's final exam was a 95 percent. I had a solid B in her class, and I calculated in class one day that in order to move from a B to an A, I would have to score a 97 percent on the final exam. I also determined that I had such a solid B that I could earn a zero on the final and still keep my B. Being the ever-so-motivated high school junior, I shrugged my shoulders and lamented to a buddy that I'd settle for the B.

Ms. McClain overheard. For the next five minutes, Ms. McClain gave me the biggest guilt trip of my life.

"This is the moment, Brassell," she said. "This is the moment that determines your entire future. This is the moment that tells us who you are and all that you will ever become."

Boy, did she know how to get under a person's skin. I studied my butt off to keep her off my back. For the next three weeks, I read and reviewed and studied with flashcards, and I scored a 96 percent on her final exam, the highest score a student had ever received on her final.

And she gave me the B. This woman frustrated me to no end. I could have killed her, but I respected her too much.

Ms. McClain was a New York Yankees fan, and she told me about Joe DiMaggio. In his last season as a Yankee, she said, DiMaggio played in a meaningless game at Yankee Stadium. The Yankees had already clinched the pennant and were ahead in a game when DiMaggio hit a single and tried to stretch it into a double. He slid face-first into second and made it safely. After the inning, a rookie asked DiMaggio why he had done it, and DiMaggio looked sternly at the rookie and said, "Because it may be some kid's first time at Yankee Stadium, and I want him to know what kind of player I am."

Ms. McClain looked at me and warned me never to put my name on anything that did not represent my greatest effort because "your worst day will always be the day you are evaluated, so make your worst day your best day." That was a heck of a lesson to learn in high school.

Steve Taylor was the reason I became a journalism major in college. I attended American University in Washington, D.C., for my undergraduate degree. I was majoring in political science when I took Taylor's journalism class. A lot of athletes took his class, so I figured it was an easy A.

After reading one of my stories, he asked me if I was a journalism major. Without waiting for my response, he added, "You know, you're one of the best writers I've ever had in my class."

That comment got me to switch majors.

What I learned from all my teachers is that teachers make a difference every day in the ways they conduct lessons, the enthusiasm they bring to their subjects, and the comments they make to their students.

Five Ways to Use This Chapter

I talk about my own teaching and learning experiences because I have found that the best way to become a better teacher is to reflect on both what worked and what didn't work for me as a student. In this way, I developed my own teaching style.

This book is meant to inspire you to become the best teacher possible. Steve Taylor, the professor who inspired me to switch majors, once told me that in order to be a great writer, you need to get readers to laugh, to cry, and to think. Training teachers at the university and in seminars across the country, I have learned that the best way for teachers to improve their approaches is to engage them in thinking about their own teaching and learning experiences. I hope you benefit from the following tips:

1. **Think about the best and worst teachers you had as a student.**

    In your eyes, what made a teacher exemplary or excruciating? How can you incorporate positive traits of great teachers into your own teaching, and how can you avoid negative characteristics of poor teachers? What is your teaching philosophy or style?

2. **Watch as many teachers as you can.**

    One of the things I advise my student teachers and beginning teachers to do at the university is to watch as many teachers as they can. If you can watch 500 teachers, you will learn more about teaching than you could from any course or book. I understand that it is not always easy to observe teachers in their classrooms, so I advise you to seek inspiration in other places as well. If you cannot observe actual classrooms, check out websites that provide teaching tips. I have watched hundreds of beneficial teaching-related videos on YouTube that have improved the way I present information to students.

Read about great teachers. I have included an abbreviated list of some of the books that inspired my teaching practices. Within these books are tons of ideas that I have "liberated" and incorporated into my classroom to benefit my own students. (I never steal an idea from a fellow teacher; I liberate their ideas.) And for those teachers who are "lazy readers" (myself included), I encourage you to watch television programs or movies that feature great teachers. I have included an abbreviated list in this chapter of some of my favorite teaching movies.

3. Write a letter to a teacher who made a difference in your life.

I have asked students in my teacher education classes to do this as an assignment, and many considered it to be the single-best activity of their teacher preparation programs. There is something powerful about writing to an influential teacher, and it is even more powerful when you receive a reply. What would you say to a teacher who made a difference in your life?

4. Start a book club at your school.

The purpose of this activity is to get to know your colleagues. You can learn from everybody at your school.

I was the union representative at one of the schools I taught in, and the position gave me the opportunity to get to know all the teachers at my school (each, inevitably, had some sort of problem they wanted me to help solve). One of the best ways I have learned to work with others is to approach them and ask for their help. Everybody wants to feel important, and I have found that my best relationships with fellow teachers have developed from me asking for their assistance in some way.

5. Help out your colleagues.

Whenever I volunteered to help my colleagues, my life became much easier at school. If you notice that another teacher is having a bad day, why not tell him or her to take a break while you fill in on playground duty? Help colleagues bring materials to and from their cars, and share materials and activities that have proven useful to you. The teachers who hoard materials and wait for others to do everything for them always tend to be the most miserable people in the school (and their students reflect that attitude).

Some Favorite Inspirational Books for Teachers

Many teachers who have attended my seminars have asked about books that may prove helpful or inspirational to them in their daily lives. The following texts are some of my personal favorites:

Aurandt, Paul. *Paul Harvey's the Rest of the Story.* New York: Bantam, 1984.

Braithwaite, E. R. *To Sir, with Love.* New York: Pyramid Books, 1967.

Carnegie, Dale. *How to Win Friends and Influence People* (reissue). New York: Pocket Books, 1990.

Codell, Esmé R. *Educating Esmé: Diary of a Teacher's First Year.* Chapel Hill, NC: Algonquin Books, 2001.

Collins, Marva, and Civia Tamarkin. *Marva Collins' Way.* New York: Jeremy P. Tarcher/Putnam, 1990.

Conroy, Pat. *The Water Is Wide.* New York: Houghton Mifflin, 1972.

Cullinan, Bernice E. *Read to Me: Raising Kids Who Love to Read.* New York: Scholastic, 1992.

Esquith, Rafe. *There Are No Shortcuts*. New York: Anchor Books, 2004.

Feynman, Richard P. *Surely You're Joking, Mr. Feynman: Adventures of a Curious Character*. New York: W. W. Norton & Co, 1985.

Fox, Mem. *Reading Magic: Why Reading Aloud to Our Children Will Change Their Lives Forever*. San Diego, CA: Harvest Original, 2001.

Freedom Writers, The, with Erin Gruwell. *The Freedom Writers Diary: How a Teacher and 150 Teens Used Writing to Change Themselves and the World Around Them*. New York: Broadway Books, 1999.

Fulghum, R. *All I Really Need to Know I Learned in Kindergarten*. New York: Ballantine, 1989.

Hill, Napoleon. *Think and Grow Rich*. New York: Fawcett Crest, 1960.

Johnson, LouAnne. *My Posse Don't Do Homework*. New York: St. Martin's Press, 1994.

Kohl, Herbert. *36 Children*. New York: Plume, 1967.

Kotlowitz, Alex. *There Are No Children Here: The Story of Two Boys Growing Up in the Other America*. New York: Nan A. Talese/ Doubleday, 1991.

Kozol, Jonathan. *Savage Inequalities*. New York: Crown Publishers, 1991.

Krashen, Stephen. *The Power of Reading*. 2nd ed. Portsmouth, NH: Heinemann, 2004.

McCourt, Frank. *Teacher Man: A Memoir*. New York: Scribner, 2005.

Nash, Jennie. *Raising a Reader: A Mother's Tale of Desperation and Delight*. New York: St. Martin's Press, 2003.

Peale, Norman Vincent. *The Power of Positive Thinking.* New York: Fawcett Crest, 1952.

Robbins, Anthony. *Unlimited Power: The New Science of Personal Achievement* (reprint). New York: Fireside, 1997.

Trelease, Jim. *The Read-Aloud Handbook.* 6th ed. New York: Penguin Books, 2006.

Some Favorite Inspirational Movies for Teachers

A lot of people (myself included) are lazy readers and can't find the time to read great books about teachers. No need to worry, as there are a number of great movies about inspirational teachers. The following is a list of my favorite movies about teaching (please note that *Dead Poets Society* is not one of them, and you may email me via my website, **www.lazyreaders.com**, to find out why):

- *Akeelah and the Bee*

- *Bill & Ted's Excellent Adventure*

- *Conrack*

- *Country Teachers* (Chinese)

- *Dangerous Minds*

- *Driving Miss Daisy*

- *Goodbye, Mr. Chips*

- *Hoosiers*

- *The Karate Kid*

- *Kindergarten Cop*

- *Lean on Me*

- *Matilda*

- *The Miracle Worker*

- *Mr. Holland's Opus*

- *My Fair Lady*

- *The Prime of Miss Jean Brodie*

- *Remember the Titans*

- *Rocky*

- *School of Rock*

- *Spellbound* (Documentary)

- *Stand and Deliver*

- *Summer School*

- *To Be and To Have* (French)

- *To Sir, With Love*

For Reflection

What did you find helpful in this chapter? Think of at least one action item you gleaned from it. A lot goes into evaluating what makes a teacher good or bad. Some of it is objective, but some of it is subjective. Will all students relate equally to your particular personality and style? How can you be sensitive to and compensate for these subjective factors?

Chapter 2

Good Parenting Is Underrated

It all starts at home.

I cannot remember if it was Socrates or Keanu Reeves who once said, "It takes a license to fish and a license to drive a car, but any idiot can become a parent." Well, now that I am a parent, I can attest that certainly has proven to be true. In defense of parents, though, nobody hands you a manual when you get your kid at the hospital. Parenting consists of a lot of trial and error, and I believe one of our responsibilities as teachers is to help educate parents on ways to best assist their children.

My appreciation for parents has grown as I've grown older. To paraphrase Mark Twain, when I was 18, my parents did not know anything, and when I was 21, I couldn't believe how much they had learned in three years. Now that I am a parent, I appreciate all that my parents did for me so much more. My parents are magnificent people. They are also an odd couple. My father is like "Rain Man," and my mother is an actress.

Growing up, I always saw my father sitting in his recliner with a glass of scotch beside him while he listened to an opera on his headset and read a book. Meanwhile, my mother, brother, sister, and I would be talking with the television set on. Now that I am a father, I truly appreciate why my father had that glass of scotch constantly by his side.

My mother talks all the time. Friends and acquaintances do not have to think too hard to guess whom I take after. When people ask why I talk so much, my response is that I never had a chance to speak growing up. Mom has never received a piece of mail that she did not think everyone in the room needed to hear her read aloud.

"Say, Danny," she'd begin. "You remember Mrs. Hufnagel? She died four years before you were born? Well, I got a letter from her daughter." She'd then proceed to read this entire letter to me, a letter that I had no interest in whatsoever. She'd read newspaper articles aloud as well.

"Say, Danny," she'd say. "Did you read about the Broncos yesterday?"

"Uh-huh."

"John Elway threw four touchdowns," she'd say, excitement building in her voice. "Did you see that?"

"Yes, Mom. I read the article."

"The defense held the Raiders to a field goal. Did you read that?"

"Yes, Mom."

"Sammy Winder carried for 123 yards. Did you see that?"

"Mom, I read the article. I saw the game on TV, too."

All the while, Mom would get more and more animated as she spoke, as if she were about to surprise me with some fact that I had not noticed. It drove me crazy, but now I realize that not only was my mother a genius, she was a saint. She did not give a hoot about football, but she knew my brother and I were addicted to all things pigskin. She learned whatever she could about football so that she could talk to us about something we were interested in. That's what exceptional mothers do. If their sons love football, they learn about football; if their sons cannot get enough of stamp collecting, they learn about stamps. For the record, though, my mother is better than yours.

People used to ask my mom why she didn't have a dishwasher. "I have three," she'd reply. "Danny, Jim, and Liz." When we washed and dried the dishes every night, our mom would sit and talk to us and read aloud anything she had handy, despite our protests. Observing my parents, I realized that you do not need a doctorate in child psychology to be a great parent. All you need to remember are a few basic tricks. If more parents practiced just a few simple exercises, our students (for that matter, our teachers and administrators as well) would be much better off. Here are some of my simple tricks to share with the parents of your students:

1. Read in front of your kids.

I cannot remember a time when I have seen either of my parents without something to read. President Reagan once said that one of his greatest fears in life would be to get stuck in a hotel room with nothing to read. My parents always have something to read with them.

It was easy for my father. He is a librarian. He always brought tons of books home. It's no secret that one of the best variables to look at when predicting student achievement is the "number of books present in the home." Take a guess at which students do better in school: the ones with a limited number of books at home or those with plentiful reading materials? My parents were never wealthy, but we always had a treasure trove of books in our home, courtesy of our library cards.

My parents always had a newspaper subscription. I can remember my father encouraging my interest in comic strips like *Peanuts* and *Blondie*. Before I could read the newspaper myself (and even after I could), my mother would read aloud news and feature stories, movie reviews, and recipes from the newspaper.

Mom likes mysteries, and she plows through them with the urgency of a first grader in need of the bathroom. She could probably start her own bookstore, coffee shop, or youth hostel with the number of used paperback mysteries she has accumulated over the years. I always heard her talking to my father about what she was reading, too.

Dad reads everything: biographies, histories, popular fiction. I guess, as a librarian, he reads partly as a homework assignment, but most of his reading is for pleasure. He has this compulsive disorder about not writing in books. Throughout my childhood, I recall my father reading and taking notes on index cards. I have no idea what he did with those cards, but he could probably create his own card catalog simply with his notes.

This is what I learned from my parents that I'd like to share with you: Kids aren't stupid. They watch everything adults do. So much of what students learn is not taught; it's caught. If kids do not see their parents read, they are not going to read. When I speak to fathers at literacy training seminars, I ask them if they wonder why their sons are so into sports. One of the primary reasons is that the only time many fathers spend with their children is when they are watching sports on television. If they read in front of and aloud to their children, their kids would be more excited about reading.

And here is a mantra to remember: It does not matter what you read, only how much you read. People who read more, read better. It does not matter if you like reading James Joyce or *James and the Giant Peach* (1961). I sit on an airplane at least once a week, and I cannot remember the last time I sat next to someone reading Molière, Shakespeare, or Dostoevsky. But I sit beside plenty of people reading *USA Today*, *People* magazine, or John Grisham books. Read in front of your kids to show them that reading is fun.

2. Eat dinner together as a family.

It may sound old-fashioned, but it is essential to eat dinner (or another meal) together as a family. I know—many families have awkward work schedules. The days of Beaver Cleaver are over. Today, June would be forced to work, and Wally and the Beaver would be latchkey kids subsisting on microwaveable junk food. Still, it is essential that nothing prevent families from gathering at some point in their day simply to talk.

Talk is not cheap. On the contrary, talk, or a lack thereof, can be very expensive. Researchers have found that children who are exposed to more talk have vastly superior vocabularies entering school than their abandoned counterparts, and this discrepancy in early elementary school just widens in subsequent years. (Two researchers at the University of Kansas, Betty Hart and Todd Risley, wrote about their eye-opening findings in this field in their seminal work, *Meaningful Differences in the Everyday Experience of Young American Children* 1995.)

What should parents talk about with their children? It matters little. Probably the best advice I can give is to rip off a lesson learned from my own mother: find out whatever your children are interested in and talk about that. Researchers have shown that it is not as important what you talk about so much as that you talk at all with your children. It is important that parents take time to speak with their children each day. If you feel awkward just talking, share an experience with your children, like playing a game.

3. Play games with your children.

During my childhood, I do not remember any time spent in the car that didn't involve my parents playing games with us.

"Hey, there goes a Volkswagen Bug," my mom would say before smacking me in the arm.

We'd pay attention to road signs and distances. My dad would point out different states' license plates. My parents would even get me to pay attention to the word environment around me.

"What sound does your name start with, Danny?"

"Dddd … "

"Good, now point to signs that start with a 'd' sound."

"Dunkin' Donuts," I'd shout and wave my hand. "Dairy Queen!" What can I say? I was a rather large child, so fast food captured my attention.

My parents always played board games and card games with my brother, sister, and me. Our hallway closets were packed with dominoes, Chutes and Ladders, Connect Four, Cootie, Candy Land, Battleship, Risk, Uno—an interactive dream world for a child. Some of my fondest childhood memories consist of nights spent playing board games at home with my family.

Again, my parents did not have any special training. They just engaged in simple activities that earned them two children who became productive adults—and me. Any parent could do the same. There is one additional activity that I want to share with you, which will hopefully motivate you to enjoy the moments you have with your children while you are still the most important people in their lives.

4. Have a "party night" with your family.

My father used to get paid every Friday. My family did not have a lot of money, but I was too young to understand that. What I did know was that every Friday meant a special trip to the grocery store with Mom.

Mom allowed each of us kids to pick out one special item for our party. I always picked out a big bag of chips, my brother always grabbed a tub of chocolate ice cream, and my sister always snagged a bunch of asparagus (incidentally, she now works for the federal government). Mom would make cheeseburgers (unless it was Lent, which meant tomato soup and grilled cheese sandwiches or, preferably, macaroni and cheese with fish stick sandwiches), the television would be turned off for the evening, and we would play board games or have sock fights or tell ghost stories.

Whoever coined the term *quality family time* stole the phrase from my parents. They are as special to me as you are to your own children. Keep this in mind: You have a tremendous home-field advantage. Nobody is as important to a young child as mommy and daddy. You lay the foundation that all of your children's future teachers will build upon.

Seven Cool Ways to Get Parents More Involved in Your Classroom

One of my mentors was a wonderful elderly Jewish lady named Estelle who would waddle into my classroom occasionally with a huge grin on her face and shout with pure glee, "Hello, boys and girls!" Whatever control I may have had over my students would go out the window the moment she entered my classroom, but I always found myself delighted to see her.

"Oh, Daniel," Estelle would practically sing, "You're dressed so nicely. Oh, and look at these lovely bulletin boards. I love how you've arranged the children's desks. May I make a suggestion?"

Now I ask you, am I going to listen to this woman's advice? You're darn right I'm going to listen to her. The woman just gave me three compliments. In contrast, my principal, who I referred to as Mrs. Lucifer, would drop by to do her daily write-up of what I was doing wrong and announce so all my students could hear her, "Let me tell you why you're not cutting it as a teacher."

My mentor was a peach. She also shared wisdom that I took to heart. At the end of every year, I write down three to five things I do well as a teacher and three to five things that I need to improve upon. At the end of my first year, I knew that I was good at inspiring students to get excited about school and to be proud of their efforts. I also realized that the most glaring need I had to address in year two was increasing parental involvement in my classroom.

Naturally, I turned to Estelle for help, and Estelle told me something that I will never forget. "Daniel," she'd say, enunciating every syllable as if she were a judge on the high bench, "You need to understand that a lot of your students' parents had negative experiences in school when they were younger, so you need to be extra sensitive and make them feel welcome."

By the end of my second year, I considered parental involvement one of my greatest strengths. Here are some suggestions on how to draw parents into your classroom to support their children's learning:

1. Three-to-One

When I was teaching second grade my second year, I had 33 students, and I vowed to call seven parents a night. Over a five-day period, I would cover all of my students. When I called, I employed what Estelle called a "three-to-one" technique. Estelle emphasized sugar over vinegar, since all parents want to hear nice things about their children. So I set a rule that I would have at least three positive contacts with a parent before I ever discussed anything negative. The first month went something like this:

Week 1 Phone Call: "Hello, Mrs. Rodriguez. This is Mr. Brassell. I just wanted to tell you that Diego has been on time to class every day this week, and he helps me clean erasers every day. I am so happy to have him in my classroom, and I thank you for all your support. If you ever need anything, please feel free to call me at home." (Many people are shocked that I would give parents my home telephone number, but I never found that parents abused it. I received fewer than 20 calls a year at home from parents.)

Week 2 Phone Call: "Hello, Mrs. Rodriguez. This is Mr. Brassell again. I just wanted to tell you that Diego won our class 100-yard dash today. I just thought you'd like to know that we may have a future Olympian on our hands. I am so happy to have him in my classroom, and I thank you for all your support. If you ever need anything, please feel free to call me at home."

Week 3 Phone Call: "Hello, Mrs. Rodriguez. This is Mr. Brassell again. I just wanted to tell you that Diego aced his spelling bee today, and he helped his table win Table of the Day. He is so well liked by his classmates and such a leader that I think he may be a future president or CEO. I am so happy to have him in my classroom, and I thank you for all your support. If you ever need anything, please feel free to call me at home."

Week 4 Phone Call: "Hello, Mrs. Rodriguez. This is—"

"Mr. Brassell," Mrs. Rodriguez interrupted. "It's so good to hear from you."

This is when I know I have her on my side. Now I can discuss any areas of concern in a way that makes Mrs. Rodriguez more inclined to listen and assist me rather than ignore me and turn defensive.

"I just want to make sure everything is all right at home," I'd tell Mrs. Rodriguez, "because Diego got in a little fight today, and I do not want this to hurt his future political ambitions because you know how the press can be."

The point is, teachers need parents on their side. Teachers do not get to choose their students or their parents.

2. Friday Family Workshops

Every Friday, I would host a workshop in my classroom for family members interested in assisting their children in various ways. To ensure attendance, I supplied soda and chips the first few weeks. Extended families showed up at the mention of free snacks, but eventually the families started bringing their own dishes, and we enjoyed community potlucks where parents could discuss their various concerns and ask each other or me any questions they had. In this way, my classroom acted as a mini community center, which was precisely my goal. I chose the topics the first few weeks but later turned over the reins to the parents. These weekly gatherings were extremely successful and positive experiences for all involved.

3. Homework Pacts

Nothing put me in a fouler mood than starting the day encountering a student who had failed to do his or her homework. My solution to this problem? Every Monday, I gave each student the week's homework along with a sheet with the days of the week listed. Every night, parents simply signed their name next to the day of the week that they worked on the homework with their children. I placed the responsibility on the parents, and my class boosted its homework completion rate to nearly 100 percent. I kept files of these sheets for each student, and I never assigned more than 30 minutes of homework on any given night.

4. Parent Autographs

I trained my students to swarm any parent visitors who entered our classroom. Whenever a parent entered our room, my students would clamor around the visitor with pencils and paper in hand, asking that parent for an autograph. How do you think you'd feel if you entered a room where everyone adored you? Would you be more likely to return? Boosting parental involvement, in my experience, is just an application of one of my favorite child psychology tricks.

5. The Board by the Door

Create a chart by the door that lists every student's name (for example, Ronaldo's parents, Cynthia's parents, Lakesha's parents, etc.). Every time a student's parent visits the classroom, place a sticker next to that student's name. I do this and I never have to say a word to the kids. I don't have to—they figure it out all by themselves.

"Mom," Ronaldo would whine. "I only got three stickers! Cynthia's got 10. You gotta come around more."

Keep in mind that not all parents can make it to your classroom during working hours, so create a system where students can earn stickers for other contributions their parents make (for example, Nestor's mother earned her son five stickers for making enchiladas for the class; Tyrell's father earned his son 10 stickers for coming in on a Saturday to help me install new bulletin boards).

6. Sticky-Note Motivators

If you need sticky notes, I suggest you ask around at doctors' offices, since they receive tons of free sticky notes from pharmaceutical companies. Whenever I need something from the community, I (1) ask, and (2) write a thank-you letter. Besides, whenever you tell someone you're a teacher, they look at you like you just told them you have a disease.

"What do you do for a living?" people inquire.

"I'm a teacher," I reply, and their smile evaporates and is replaced by a look of discomfort.

"Really?" they'll say. "That's great. Go get 'em," and they'll ease away from you as if you were contagious.

Anyhow, I get all these sticky notes from doctors' offices, and then I distribute them to parents to write notes of encouragement to their children to post on our Sticky-Note Motivation Board. Kids get a kick out of seeing notes of encouragement and praise from loved ones. (You can also write elected officials, athletes, and other celebrities and ask them to write words of encouragement to your students.)

7. Parent Recordings

I also give parents cassette tapes to record messages of encouragement to their children. You can get cassettes very cheaply at discount stores, and you can send students home with tape recorders for parents who do not have them. Depending on the resources available at your school, there are many other ways to record electronic messages. I found that my Friday workshops in my classroom were good times to encourage parents to make recordings, if they could not do it at home.

For Reflection

Reflect for a moment on why parental involvement is so important in your classroom. Which of these tips would work best for you? Think of some other ways you have been able to boost the participation of parents in your class.

Chapter 3

Passion Is Powerful

Stand up right now and repeat after me: I love to teach!

Now wave your arms wildly and give yourself a hoot and a holler. Bring this book to school, stand in front of your students, and lead them in this chant:

> (You say) Who? Who? Who's the best?
>
> (Students say) We're! We're! We're the best!
>
> (You say) Who's the best?
>
> (Students say) We're the best!
>
> (Everybody says) On all tests!

Get pumped up about teaching. Love what you do and you'll never work a day in your life. No matter how corny it may sound, your vocation should be like a vacation. The people who are jazzed about teaching teach better and longer.

Why did you become a teacher? I am going to go out on a limb and suggest it was not for the high pay or heaps of praise constantly bestowed on teachers. (If you teach in a school district that provides these, please send me the address.) I bet you became a teacher for the opportunity to make a difference in the lives of children.

Samuel Taylor Coleridge said that "nothing is so contagious as enthusiasm." If you're enthusiastic about the things you are working on, people will ask you to do interesting things. People feel your passion, and students certainly feel your passion for teaching. Good teachers passionately pursue excellence.

Remember the old Chinese proverb: a person without a smiling face must not open a shop. What does that mean? If you're having a bad week in the classroom, please remember these two simple words: sick day. Take a day off. Go to the mall. Try not to discipline other people's children while you are there. Treat yourself to a nice meal. Watch a movie. Read a book! The next day, you are going to return to school feeling reinvigorated. Your students will feel re-energized and jazzed to see you. And I don't know about you, but whenever I took a sick day (also known among teachers as a mental health day), I requested the crankiest substitute to fill in for me. I wanted my students to be begging to get me back.

Your passion is reflected in everything you do. We need you to teach for a long time, and the more you incorporate your passion into the classroom, the more likely you are to keep teaching for a long time. I've observed thousands of teachers, and it usually takes me less than a minute to pinpoint a teacher's interests. If Ms. Thompson's students are always singing, it's very likely that Ms. Thompson likes music. If Mrs. Pierce's students seem to conduct a lot of science experiments, my guess would be that Mrs. Pierce enjoys science.

For years, I have attended workshops and trainings that have emphasized that we remember:

- 10% of what we read
- 20% of what we hear
- 30% of what we see
- 50% of what we see and hear
- 70% of what we discuss
- 80% of what we experience
- 95% of what we teach someone else

The funny thing about these numbers is that they are completely bogus. They are based on Dale's Cone of Experience (Dale 1969), which attempted to illustrate the effectiveness of audio-visual media. Dale never offered any research to support his claims, and the numbers that have been attributed to his "cone of experience" were made up by others. Regardless, I like the idea, so I have always emphasized to my students that our goal is to spend the bulk of our learning time experiencing new things, discussing these experiences, and reteaching our experiences to others. We need to be passionate about learning. My favorite quote about passion comes from Pablo Picasso. He said, "If they took away all my paints, I'd use pastels. If they took away my pastels, I'd use crayons. If they took away my crayons, I'd use a pencil. If they put me in a cell and stripped me of everything, I'd spit on my finger and draw on the wall." Dang! That dude loved to paint! There wasn't anything that anyone could do to prevent Picasso from pursuing his passion. What a terrific example for all of us to follow.

I spend too much time away from my family while speaking at seminars across the country. One of the things I do to remind my wife that I'm thinking of her while I'm away is to place "love notes" for her throughout the house. For students, I place notes of encouragement in their books. For example, I'll leave a signed note in one of Efraim's books that says, "Efraim—I love the way you share books with your tablemates." Or I'll leave a signed note in Laura's desk that says, "Laura—I love how clean you keep your desk." I want kids to be as excited about finding the notes as I am about writing them.

Anyone who knows me knows that I am passionate about reading, and I strive to turn students into passionate readers. To do this, I need my students to come to school. When I discovered that Tuesdays had the lowest attendance of the week, I came up with Terrific Tuesdays.

When students came into the classroom on Tuesday mornings, they would rush to their desks to find books. Each book had a sticky note attached with a personalized message like "Rachelle—I know how much you love horses. Enjoy this book about horses. Love, The Book Fairy." Students would jump up in the air, clinging to their books and yelling, "The Book Fairy came! The Book Fairy came!" Once I started leaving books from the Book Fairy, attendance in my class on Tuesdays skyrocketed to almost 100 percent. More importantly, my students were smiling, excited, and sharing their books and notes with one another.

Turn your weaknesses into your strengths. I cherish and embrace the daily challenges that teaching brings.

Seven Tips for Igniting Your Passion

All of us need to light our fires from time to time. My goal as someone who trains teachers is to retain teachers for as long as possible. In his wonderful book *All I Really Need to Know I Learned in Kindergarten*, author Robert Fulghum points out the importance of living a balanced life: "Learn some and think some and draw and paint and sing and dance and play and work every day some" (1989). Here are some ideas to keep you excited in the classroom:

1. Daily Laugh

I told my students that according to a Harvard study (whenever I cite research, I always say that Harvard conducted the study, as it sounds much more legitimate that way), the average adult laughs approximately 15 times a day, while the average kindergartener laughs 300 times a day. I instructed them that their job was to make me laugh at least 315 times a day. Every day I would tell jokes and riddles from silly books and websites, show silly film and TV clips (YouTube is amazing), and play funny songs on my aging tape recorder or antique record player (my school was at the cutting edge of technology—nineteenth-century technology, that is).

2. Daily Doodle

Encourage your students to doodle. Doodling helps many learners stay focused on lessons. I share my doodles from faculty meetings with students, and I even post student doodles on our "Abstract Thinking" bulletin board. I love getting kids to doodle and then explain to the class what they were thinking while they doodled. This is a great way to encourage student reflection and for me to see what students find meaningful in my lectures. Oh, and I like to color, too!

3. Sing It!

I love to sing. I am not a very good singer, and that is precisely why I sing with my students every day (yes, I even sing with my middle school and high school students). Students need to see teachers take risks, and I learned long ago to leave my pride at the door. We have a standing policy in my class that if students can create a song or chant that teaches a learning standard, we earn an extra read aloud or free reading time. I have found that anything can be taught through music. Here are a couple of samples (attend one of my workshops and I'll show you the gestures that go with each song):

Seven Continents
(to the beat of "Frère Jacques")

There are seven—
There are seven—
Continents.
Continents.
Europe, Asia, Africa—
North and South America—
Antarctica.
Australia.

Parts of a Plant
(to the beat of "Whoomp! There It Is")

Flower, leaves, stem—
Roots! There it is!

Place Value with 142
(to the beat of "Bibbidi-Bobbidi-Boo")

Look at the hundreds spot.
Look at the tens spot.
Look at the ones spot, too.
Put them together, and what do you get?
One hundred forty-two!

4. Brain Teasers

I love solving puzzles. Yes, I am the kind of person who likes to guess who committed the murder (maybe it developed from playing the board game Clue when I was young). Every day I like to throw out different problems for my students to try and solve. This activity keeps me young, because I appreciate students explaining their rationales. Activities can range from listing seven American cities that begin with the letter *S* to explaining how to keep a dog from eating one's homework. I love presenting problems to students and discussing alternative solutions. I have learned that there is almost always more than one right answer when approaching problems from multiple points of view.

5. Jingle Jangle

I have about as much rhythm as a rabid dog, but nothing seems to relax my students and me more than getting up out of our seats and dancing. Maybe we'll spell out words in a "Y.M.C.A."-like fashion, or maybe we'll speed up the moves of "Waddle Le Ah Cha." Dancing with students is a great way to get them (and you) to smile and to stimulate blood to the brain. A little bit of dancing can go a long way toward learning.

6. Show-and-Tell

Bring back show-and-tell. You might have to rename it "standardized, research-based sharing activity," but it is essential for students to have an opportunity to share their lives with one another. Why? Human beings are naturally nosy. That's why reading journals have subscription rates in the thousands, while tabloids boast subscription rates in the millions. Most people care more about what their favorite celebrities are up to than how to teach kids to read. While my students may ignore *me* throughout the day, I know they are paying attention to their classmates during show-and-tell. They want to know about one another, and I'd like to get to know more about them as well.

7. Just for You

Finally, you need to know how great you are, and if you are waiting for others to tell you, you may be in for a long wait. Reward yourself at least once a week for a job well done. A friend of mine reminded me that work will always be there for me, so I should always keep work *there*. Translation: Try not to take your work home with you. I am an early bird, so I get to school early to get work done. A lot of teachers stay after school to get things done. Do whichever works best for you, but taking my friend's advice was one of the best things I ever did. I try to always keep work at work so that my family gets 100 percent of my attention when I'm at home. Zig Ziglar, the famous motivational speaker, said that most people think about work when they are with their families and their families when they are at work, and they wind up never being anywhere. The best way to preserve your passion is to stay fresh, and the best way to stay fresh is to maintain a work-life balance.

For Reflection

What did you find useful in this chapter? Think of an action item to integrate into your daily or weekly routine. Think back to your first day of teaching, or before. What was it that excited you and inspired you? Think of the things that you are passionate about in your personal life. Are there one or two of those passions that you have not incorporated into your classroom that would help energize you?

We Become Whom We Hang Out With

Ever lean on wet paint? It rubs off on you, doesn't it? It's the same with people. So why would you ever choose to hang out with negative people?

I always advise students, parents, and friends to avoid what I call "toxic teachers." These folks are the worrywarts who whine and complain about everything. They are not much different than the kids in every class who always whine and tattle. Toxic teachers are the kings and queens of excuses. Their complaints are endless.

"I teach the poor kids."

"My kids don't speak English."

"My kids have nothing to read at home."

"My back hurts."

If you want to avoid toxic teachers, my advice to you is to avoid the teachers' lounge, as these refuges are petri dishes for complaints.

When I was teaching elementary school in Compton, California, one of my favorite activities after a long day of teaching was attending mandatory professional development sessions with teachers from my school district. I would walk in the room, and teachers would look at me with concern and query, "What's the matter, Mr. Brassell?"

I'd stare and confess, "I had a student pull a knife on me today."

Then a woman would put a hand on her hip, shake her head, and brag, "Honey, I had a kid pull a gun on me today."

Then a guy in the corner would offer, "I had a kid pull out a hand grenade and blow up half my classroom."

"You have a classroom?" another teacher would ask incredulously. "I have to teach my students on the grass."

"At least you've got grass at your school," another teacher would say, stunned. "We've only got gravel at my school."

I called it "Compton One-Upmanship" because I learned that no matter what problems I thought I had as a teacher, there was always someone who had it worse. I am reminded of what Lou Holtz, the football coach, used to say—"Don't tell your problems to people: eighty percent don't care; and the other twenty percent are glad that you have them."

In order to maintain your sanity, you need to surround yourself with positive influences. That's not always an easy thing to do at a school site.

When I first started teaching, I was so eager to impress my students. I'd always show up at school around 4 or 5 A.M., hop the fence, and break into my classroom. (I didn't have the key, so my kids showed me how to jimmy the lock.) Every day I wanted to make 10 new decorations for the class. I wanted my kids to think my class was cooler than Disneyland. Every day at school would seem to start the same. I'd be in my classroom making games and decorations for my kids. I was wired on coffee and anxious to start teaching. I had a smile plastered from ear to ear; I was so excited for the kids to show up.

And then the first bell would ring, and I'd make my way to the playground to get the kids. Walking across the yard to the cafeteria, the janitor would tell me that one of my boys had urinated all over the bathroom. I'd shake my head and say I'd talk to him.

And then I'd walk through the cafeteria, and a cook would tell me a couple of my girls had been throwing corn dogs at each other during breakfast. So I'd apologize and continue on my way.

Then I'd walk toward the office, and a parent would start screaming in Spanish that her little *niño* was getting bullied by a fifth grader, and I should tell her boy to hit back. So I'd tell her to calm down, and I would talk to her son, the fifth-grade bully, and the bully's teacher.

Then I'd make it to the office to pick up my attendance sheet. Before my hand could leave my mailbox, the secretary would tell me to get my attendance form back earlier or I could expect a late paycheck. So I'd apologize and continue on my way to the playground.

Then the principal would stop me and tell me that I might as well stop asking for supplies because the school didn't have any money. So I'd shrug and continue on my way. By the time I finally reached the kids, my smile had completely disappeared, and I just wanted the day to end.

Fortunately, the one constant energizer in my classroom was my students. Teaching is so rewarding when you recognize the enthusiasm of your students and realize that they are depending on you. We talked about passion in the previous chapter. While passion has to come from within, it's nice to receive positive energy from others. I may not always be able to find positive people, but I make certain to avoid negative people. I once ran into a colleague who looked like she was a step away from a visit to the morgue. When I asked her how long she had been sick, she replied: "In three weeks, it will be a month." This is the single-most negative person I have ever encountered, and I made sure to avoid her at all costs. Some people are just looking to unload all their life's ills and worries on you, and you should make sure you are not a willing participant.

You need to avoid the naysayers. There are people out there who get their kicks by bringing other people down. I have learned that these miserable people are not satisfied with being miserable. They want you to feel miserable as well.

There are plenty of examples throughout history of critics who told others they could never do what they envisioned. Three come to mind:

"Who the [heck] wants to hear actors talk?" asked Harry Warner, the head of Warner Brothers Studios in 1927. Two years later, *The Jazz Singer* ushered in the age of talking motion pictures.

"There is no likelihood man can ever tap the power of the atom," Robert Millikan, who won the Nobel Prize for Physics, famously said in 1923. Less than 25 years later, scientists had developed the atom bomb.

Charles Duell, the head of the U. S. Patent Office, said in 1899, "Everything that can be invented has been invented."

Two thousand years ago, everybody knew the earth was the center of the universe. Five hundred years ago, everybody knew the earth was flat. Just a few years ago, everybody knew that real estate was the safest investment. In a world filled with people who think they know it all, it is sometimes sound advice to think on your own. Surround yourself with positives and focus on what your students can do. The possibilities are astounding.

My Five Essential Ideas for Surrounding Yourself with Positives

Would you like to know the secret to a longer life? Turn off the television news and read a funny children's book every night. I can already tell you what's on the news tonight: the world is coming to an end, and the president is doing a bad job. It has been the same negative news for the last 100 years. Now that I am a parent, I never watch the news because the first five stories are usually about missing kids.

I read funny children's books every night. In this way, I impress my friends as well. "I read a book from cover to cover last night," I'll say. "Really?" they'll reply, clearly impressed by my feat. "What was it about?" "It was about this cat in a hat," I'll reply.

Folks, I stopped taking myself seriously long ago in exchange for seriously playing, and I am a much happier and better person for it. I've managed to befriend great people, attract wonderful work associates, and maintain terrific relationships with my family members (even the nutcases). Here are some ideas for surrounding yourself with positives:

1. Tune Out Static

Avoid the naysayers. Whenever you come across a person who likes to put you down, you need to tune that person out. Speaker and author Keith Harrell says, "Garbage in, garbage stays," and I agree. Too often we listen to the opinions of others—others whom we do not even respect. Try to avoid these negative influences, and when you must be around them, let the "garbage" they say enter one ear and exit the other.

2. A Simple Trick

I know a trick that only requires two fingers. Take both of your index fingers, place them on the sides of your mouth, and push the sides of your lips upward. It is amazing how much goodwill a smile attracts. I have found that my smile acts like a repellant to Sad Sallies who mope across the face of the earth, and I notice a lot more people smiling at me when I smile at them. Try it out and pay attention to how many more people smile at you when you smile at them. Once you get really good, say hello and compliment others. Kindness does not take a lot of effort, and you will find others energizing you because of your positive energy.

3. Ask for Help

My wife once asked me to buy a watermelon at the supermarket, and I had no idea how to judge a watermelon. So, against all male instincts, I asked a gentleman to help me find a ripe watermelon. His name was Pedro, and he kindly tapped on watermelons for about three minutes before he found one that he thought would suit my wife. I probably bumped into him three more times while shopping that day, and each time, we smiled, laughed, and chatted. What I learned from that encounter was that everybody likes to feel important, and the best way to make someone feel important is to ask for his or her assistance.

I have asked colleagues for advice on how to handle discipline problems, ideas for motivating students, strategies for teaching mathematics, and help with numerous other dilemmas. Once I ask a colleague for help, this is what it leads to: they start talking to me without me initiating a conversation; they smile more often; they share supplies that they had previously been hoarding for the next nuclear war; and they make a number of other kind gestures. Even some of the grumpiest people I have ever worked with have completed a 180-degree turnaround in their conduct when I have asked for their advice. It is one of my favorite ways to keep the people around me positive.

4. Know Your Strengths

When I was hired to train teachers at California State University, Dominguez Hills, I explained to the dean that if she needed someone to teach, I could teach. If she needed somebody to write, I could write. If she needed somebody to promote the college, I could promote the college. What I could not do, I explained to her, was attend lots of meetings.

Too often, teachers are asked to be good at everything. I have found that to be very difficult. Typical elementary school teachers need to teach a wide range of curricula, and just because a person is a great teacher does not ensure that he or she is equally good at teaching language arts, mathematics, social studies, and science. My greatest weakness is that I suffer from an underappreciated condition known as "meeting narcolepsy."

Above my desk, I have a trinket that reads: If something is urgent, do it yourself. If you have time, delegate it. If you have forever, form a committee.

Colleagues have commented that one of their favorite activities is watching me at faculty meetings. I always have a smile on my face. My secret is this: I try not to pay attention to anything being said because I find meetings to be pretty useless. Now, some people love meetings and are great at committee work, and I fully appreciate those people. I encourage those people to attend lots of meetings, and they can depend on me to teach and write. I find that most hour-long meetings begin with 15 minutes of people catching up on one another's lives. The next 15 minutes revolve around a discussion on when to have the next meeting. The following 15 minutes focus on the dissemination of information I could have read in an email. And finally, the meeting ends with 15 minutes centered on a debate of a micro-issue that does not involve higher-order thinking skills.

My strategy for enduring meetings? I write songs. I doodle. I think of crazy ways to decorate my classroom. I do whatever I have to do to keep myself in a positive state of mind.

5. Make Non-Teacher Friends

I love the people I work with, and I continue to love them because I do not spend all my time with them. I have found that when you get caught up in the minutiae of your field, you become a much less interesting person. As often as possible, I try to hang out with friends who have very different professions. My wife is a dental hygienist, and I love listening to her describe her difficulties cleaning people's teeth or dealing with bad breath. It puts what I do in perspective.

For Reflection

Think of the colleagues who energize you. What can you learn from them to make sure you are someone that people want to be around? What is the best piece of advice you gleaned from this chapter?

Perspiration

Now that we've had a chance to think about what inspires us, let's look at some things we can work on in an effort to produce great lifelong learners.

Chapter 5

To Each His or Her Own

Would you like to know the secret to good teaching? Yoda told me. Actually, the secret to good teaching comes from a man by the name of Howard Gardner. He's a professor at Harvard. He's a handsome fellow and quite nice, I'm told. Dr. Gardner wrote a highly acclaimed book back in 1983 that described seven multiple intelligences. Then he wrote another book in the late 1990s that pointed out two new intelligences. While Gardner's theory of multiple intelligences is important, he actually stole his ideas from a more important educational philosopher of the late 1970s who appeared on NBC. His name, of course, is Gary Coleman.

Gary Coleman said that teachers only have to remember this one thing: different strokes for different folks. This is so important to remember that you should recite it aloud wherever you are reading this right now. Don't be shy. People will not judge you poorly. Say it out loud and say it proud: "Different strokes for different folks!"

Every kid is different. That's what makes teaching so hard. Students within the same classroom are different. Class dynamics from period to period or year to year can be completely unique. Different is OK. We should embrace differences, not avoid them. Goodness gracious, I tell my kids, if everybody were the same, our dining options would be quite limited.

They say that anyone can teach, and I completely agree. Anyone can teach. But that saying drives me nuts, because it takes a lot of hard work to be a great teacher. The other saying that really makes me go bonkers is, "If you reach just one child, you have succeeded as a teacher." I am here to tell you that if you reach just one child, please find another job. I can accidentally affect four kids. You're wasting my tax dollars if you are just affecting one kid at a time.

I love seeing what makes different students tick. Even though I was making a ton of money as a public-school teacher, I decided to take a tutoring job after school—just for the fun of it. I tutored "underachieving geniuses." Of course, I refer to almost all of my students as underachieving geniuses. I once worked one-on-one, however, with an eight-year-old child prodigy named Tyler who truly was an underachieving genius.

During our first session together, I told Tyler that I had chosen to read aloud to him *The Adventures of Huckleberry Finn* by Mark Twain. Tyler rebuked this idea, explaining that he had read the story on his own "a long time ago." I tried not to think about how I normally reserved this book for my eighth-grade students. Challenging him, I asked Tyler if he had ever heard of any stories by William Shakespeare. Tyler enthusiastically informed me that not only had he read all 37 of Shakespeare's plays (there are *that* many? I thought to myself), he preferred Shakespeare's comedies the best, like *Twelfth Night*. He then proceeded to quote his favorite passage from the play while I bit my fingernails and commented that it was my favorite part of the play as well. I noted to myself that I must read *Twelfth Night*.

"Ever read anything by the Greeks?" I queried in a way that suggested I already knew the answer to this one.

"Oh, *Oedipus*, *Medea*," he began to list, and at this point, beads of sweat trickled down my forehead. I hate it when my students are smarter than I am, especially when they still have most of their baby teeth.

Tyler taught me one of the best lessons I have learned as a teacher: humility. Everybody is smarter than I am—about something. We each possess unique knowledge, and we each have our own ways of processing that information. Everybody learns in different ways. Everybody favors a certain strategy.

Tyler learned best through movement. He could come up with a movement for every concept, and this would help him learn it. I've always learned best through music. I think music is helpful for most of us, and I can prove it.

Can you remember the name of the 18th president of the United States? How about the capital of South Dakota? What's the largest organ in the human body? Do you know how many voting members of Congress there are? For those of you dying to know, the answers are Ulysses S. Grant, Pierre, skin, and 535.

Now let's see if you could complete any of these phrases (and feel free to hum to yourself if you'd like):

In fourteen hundred and ninety-two …

Plop, plop, fizz, fizz …

Conjunction junction …

You may have trouble remembering where you put your keys, or even the names of your own children, but you will always remember the jingles you learned in first grade. After all, in order to teach students the alphabet, all educators had to do was put it to the beat of "Twinkle, Twinkle, Little Star," and then kids learned it.

I have a philosophy: keep kids moving and playing. That is going to make them happy. When kids are happy, that's when they learn best because they do not even realize they are learning. There are lots of ways to turn kids on to school.

Dare to Differentiate: 50 Terrific Tricks for Teachers

Carol Ann Tomlinson coined the term *differentiated instruction*. In plain English, this refers to the need for teachers to consider the individual needs of each student. Taking into consideration their classroom environment, as well as student readiness, interest, and learning profiles, teachers differentiate content, adjust strategies, and vary assignments.

Here are 50 tips I train teachers to consider when differentiating instruction:

Environment

1. Create a supportive environment of mutual respect.
2. Develop a sense of community.
3. Facilitate an environment where students feel safe to take risks.
4. Promote the development of a broad range of skills and interests that incorporate all the senses.
5. Set up a physical classroom for student-centered instruction.
6. Provide purposeful materials and resources.
7. Have high expectations for all.

Readiness

8. Allow students to show what they know in a variety of ways.
9. Provide students with plenty of time to explore, understand, and transfer learning to long-term memory.
10. Give students time to revisit ideas and concepts in order to connect or extend them.
11. Ensure that lessons are developmentally appropriate.
12. Tier activities to provide an appropriate level of challenge.
13. Adapt curriculum to provide enrichment and challenge.

Interest

14. Incorporate creativity.
15. Allow students to choose what they learn, how they learn, and how they demonstrate their learning (flexible and varied).
16. Offer real-world challenges that are directly connected to the students' lives.
17. Offer novel, unique, and engaging activities to capture and sustain students' attention.
18. Use multimedia and technology.

Learning Profile

19. Focus on students' learning styles.
20. Emphasize brain-compatible instruction.
21. Recognize and honor cultural diversity.
22. Emphasize students' strengths and develop ways to compensate for weaknesses.
23. Permit positive movement (many students learn better on their toes).

Content

24. Present the curriculum through interdisciplinary "big ideas" rather than disconnected small facts.
25. Plan before, during, and after instruction.
26. Negotiate "contracts" (daily and weekly goals) with students to provide appropriate learning activities.
27. Challenge students to go a bit farther every day.
28. Create learning centers.
29. Co-develop standards with students.
30. Clearly state expectations and be specific about requirements.
31. Empower learners. Encourage students to help set and enforce norms.

Process

32. Promote active, hands-on learning.
33. Allow students to work collaboratively and independently (flexible grouping).
34. Make use of higher-level thinking and questioning strategies.
35. Give students plenty of time for reflection and goal setting.
36. Vary strategies.

Process *(cont.)*

37. Consider integrated curriculum, problem-based learning, and service learning.

38. Balance teacher-chosen and teacher-directed activities with student-chosen and student-directed activities.

39. Help students understand the group's shared needs for success (the need to belong, the need to trust, etc.)

40. Monitor student progress constantly.

41. Aim high and scaffold weaknesses.

42. Teach for meaning, not rote.

43. Be flexible with time, space, materials, and groupings.

44. Teach strategies explicitly so students have an easy way out of tough spots.

45. Collaborate with parents, resource specialists, etc. It takes a village.

Product

46. Provide opportunities for projects, creativity, problems, and challenges.

47. Focus on student growth.

48. Initiate student-maintained portfolios and assessments with varied and original products.

49. Support students in creating projects for a real audience through public displays and performances.

50. Emphasize quality of thought and expression over accuracy.

For Reflection

Consider some of the successes and failures you've had in differentiating your classroom. What have you learned from this chapter than can help you? Out of the 50 tips presented here, think about the three that will help you most. Make a plan to implement these strategies in your classroom.

Chapter 6

Reading Matters

Why don't people read? Two reasons are usually cited. First of all, there is a thing called *illiteracy*, which means people cannot read. Then, there's a thing called *aliteracy*, which means they won't read. Both are paralyzing, but I'd like to suggest that there really is no such thing as illiteracy. There are simply different degrees of literacy.

For example, when you see a red light, what does that mean? If you said stop, than you are wiser than many of the drivers I encounter in Los Angeles. What does a blue placard with a white figure in a wheelchair mean? If you said, "good parking spot," you are on a roll. We have nearly 300 DVDs in my house, but my young son and daughter can spot *Finding Nemo* no matter where I hide it. As a matter of fact, from the time they are in the womb, children can identify the golden arches of McDonald's. "Stop the car!" my children shout from the backseat whenever they see the land of Happy Meals. These are all forms of literacy, though none involve reading actual words.

Maybe the bigger challenge for our students is not the inability to read, but the lack of interest in reading. Even I suffer from a degree of aliteracy. The happiest day of my life was the day I earned my doctorate. When my wife saw me grinning from ear to ear, she asked me why I was so excited. I replied, "Because from now on, I get to pick out my own books." Whenever I need to get to sleep, I do not turn to pills. All I have to do is find a thick education textbook (one not written by me, of course) and read a few paragraphs, and that usually puts me out quicker than five margaritas.

So what's the problem? I have two ideas. First of all, there are too many things competing for attention. Kids today are too often choosing not to read.

When I speak to audiences across the country, there is always some person who cannot understand why kids these days don't like to read. "After all," this person points out, "I liked to read when I was a kid." Then I remind these people that when they were kids, fire had just been discovered. Adults need to appreciate all the things competing for students' attention. We have television shows and movies with such rapid scene changes, it's no wonder students suffer from attention deficit disorder. Students have the Internet now, where they can pop open 20 to 30 windows at a time. And there are video games with characters that are more lifelike than some of the celebrities I see in Hollywood.

We need to make reading the activity of choice for students, and that is why I emphasize to teachers and parents that I am "pro-choice." Let kids choose what they read. The research is quite clear on this—and I'm a research-based teacher. The research says that it does not matter what you read. All that matters is how much you read. I have attracted many boys and some girls to reading by handing them football cards and the sports section of the newspaper. We need to make reading the most enticing offering to our students.

Second, booklovers need more news coverage. Why is it that *Time* magazine always names a president or a terrorist as Person of the Year? How about considering one of the following two women?

TGFO. Thank God for Oprah. Have you ever heard of Oprah Winfrey? She is somebody I greatly admire, and you need to know something about me. I am a spiritual person. Every night, I say a simple prayer. I pray, "Dear Lord, please let Oprah read one of my books and just talk about it on her show." What happens when Oprah simply "talks" about a book on her show? It becomes an instant bestseller. She talks about a 75-year-old book called *Of Mice and Men* and bookstores cannot keep copies on the shelves. And, correct me if I'm wrong, but I have never seen Oprah say, "Oh! Have you read *Their Eyes Were Watching God*? Here's what I'd like you to do at home: get out a piece of paper and a pen, and write down the copyright date, the three main characters, the theme...." No! Remember these four words: traditional book reports stink! They make kids hate reading.

Oprah talks about her favorite books the same way people talk about their favorite movies or sports teams or songs. She gets people excited about reading by talking about great books.

The other woman I greatly admire is a former welfare mom by the name of J. K. Rowling, who—while stuck waiting for a train—dreamt up an entire series of adventures about a little boy named Harry Potter. The *Harry Potter* books (1997–2007), along with books like *The Adventures of Huckleberry Finn* (1885), are among the most banned books in American schools. I've learned that children have these remarkable things between their ears known as brains. Banning books is never the answer; providing students with the tools they need to select quality literature is. Whoever cannot see the value of the *Harry Potter* books (which are almost single-handedly responsible for drawing students back into bookstores) might want to actually read them. They contain one of my favorite lessons that I impart to students: you decide your own destiny by your everyday actions. By the way, I'd guess that the recently renewed interest in C. S. Lewis and *The Chronicles of Narnia* (1950–56) has a lot to do with the popularity of *Harry Potter*.

Here is a riddle: what was your favorite textbook as a child? If you are trying to decide whether it was your eighth-grade grammar book or your 11th-grade civics book, there is something seriously wrong with you. The emphasis on textbooks in this country drives me crazy. For the price of a brand-new textbook, I could purchase 15 books that would actually get kids interested in reading. One of my old principals—the one I referred to earlier—Mrs. Lucifer, once asked me if I used my textbook, and I could honestly answer that I did. They make great doorstops. But they are not the best tools to build students' interest in reading.

Let me emphasize it again: the more interested students are in reading, the more likely they are to read. The more students read, the better they get at reading. It does not take a rocket scientist to figure this out.

It is important for teachers to provide time in class for students to read. This is my Sally Struthers speech: In 10 minutes a day—the time it takes to drink a cup of coffee—you could significantly improve your students' reading levels. In all my years of teaching, I have learned that no matter what I do, I cannot control my students' home environments. I can, however, control my classroom environment. There is not a teacher in the United States who can honestly tell me that he or she cannot find at least 10 minutes in the day to allow students to read. I'd argue that those are the most important 10 minutes of any student's day because it is encouraging a lifelong habit.

It is also important for teachers and parents to read out loud to children. When should you start reading aloud to children? As soon as they are conceived. When should you stop? Never. My friend and mentor Jim Trelease has written the definitive book on reading aloud, titled *The Read-Aloud Handbook* (1982). This is the first book you should rush out and buy, after mine. He does not need me to push his book, since it has become one of the most beloved teacher/parent resources of the last 30 years (that's why there are six editions). One of the most important points he makes is that kids are not stupid. They are not going to read if they do not see adults reading, and read alouds are one of the best advertisements for how fun reading can be.

Reading should always be fun. Human beings are drawn toward pleasure-oriented activities. I'll give you an example. My wife and I were finishing dinner one night when she asked me if I wanted more green beans.

"Sorry, honey," I replied. "I am stuffed."

"We have chocolate cake for dessert," she said.

"Yum," I said. "Can I have just a small slice?"

We always find room for the things we are interested in. I want students to find room for reading every day. Let students read where they want, when they want, and with whomever they want.

Where do you like to read at home? In bed, on the sofa, on the toilet? Put these things in your classroom. (Well, maybe just the sofa or a comfy chair.) I let students read under their tables, on top of their tables, outside, on one leg—whatever works for them. Our job as teachers is to create an atmosphere that encourages our students to maximize their learning.

There is a concept in philosophy known as *Occam's razor*. It was articulated by Sir William of Occam back in the fourteenth century. Sir William of Occam discovered that the best solution to most problems is usually the simplest one. We have overcomplicated so many things in education when the simple things tend to work best. Repeat after me: the most important thing … that I can do … to help my students succeed … is to remember the 3 Rs: read … read … read.

Books That Changed My Life

There are three significant books that changed my life, and I would like to share them with you:

1. For the Fun of It: *The Pelican Brief* by John Grisham (1992)

I studied abroad in Madrid, Spain, as part of my university exchange program. While in Madrid, I learned a lot about empathy, because it was the first time I experienced discrimination.

Without doing a thing, I was born with all sorts of advantages for life in America. I was born male and white, for example. I had never experienced any sort of real discrimination until I studied in Spain. People thought I was stupid because I could not communicate very well in Spanish. It was not that I was stupid; I just did not speak or understand Spanish very well because my experiences had been limited to some high school Spanish classes.

If you have ever lived or traveled extensively in a country where people speak a different language than you, I think you can relate to what I am about to say. It is not easy to communicate in another language. I used to get headaches and experience nightmares. Spanish overwhelmed me, and I craved English wherever I could get it. A girl I went to school with loaned me her copy of John Grisham's *The Pelican Brief*, and I devoured it in a day. Then I found *A Time to Kill* and read that in a day. I found a used bookstore that sold me a battered copy of Grisham's *The Firm* and gladly paid $30 for my reading fix.

From John Grisham I graduated to books by Sydney Sheldon, Jeffrey Archer, and Ken Follett, among others. For the first time in my life, I began to read "for the fun of it." As long as somebody tells you that you have to read something, I am convinced that is not reading at all. It is only reading when we choose to do it ourselves. I want to inspire students to read for themselves.

2. Be a Hero: *Gifted Hands* by Ben Carson (1996)

I first saw Dr. Carson on *Oprah*. I watch *Oprah* because I like happy endings, and Oprah always has a happy ending.

Dr. Carson is the director of pediatric neurosurgery at Johns Hopkins University. He is the first African American to serve in that capacity there and is world famous for his work with separating conjoined twins. After watching his interview with Oprah, I rushed out to buy a copy of his autobiography.

When he was in fifth grade, Carson found himself struggling academically. His mother, a single parent raising two sons, laid down the law. She told Carson that he could not go out with his friends or watch television until he had gone to the public library and checked out two books. Each week she required him to write two book reports.

Well, Carson turned his life around and wound up graduating high school. He was accepted to a small school in New Haven, Connecticut. You may have heard of it: Yale University. After graduating from Yale, he went on to attend medical school at the University of Michigan, and from there, he found his way to Johns Hopkins, one of the most prestigious medical facilities in the world.

Here's the twist: Carson's mother, Sonya, was functionally illiterate. For years, she read Carson's book reports even though she couldn't understand them. I tell the story of Sonya Carson to parents because this is the type of person who belongs on the front page of every newspaper. Sonya Carson let nothing prevent her from raising a son who loved learning. She is a magnificent role model, the type of hero who walks among us every day and never receives the recognition she truly deserves.

3. Lifelong Learning: *The Rise of Theodore Roosevelt* by Edmund Morris (2001)

Before I read this book, I knew two things about Teddy Roosevelt: teddy bears were named after him and his face is on Mount Rushmore. I gained a significant appreciation for both Teddy Roosevelt and Edmund Morris after reading this book.

Edmund Morris won the Pulitzer Prize for this work, the first in a trilogy about Teddy Roosevelt. This book guides readers through Roosevelt's life up until the presidency. Its sequel, *Theodore Rex,* chronicles Roosevelt's presidency. I anxiously await the third book, which Morris is supposedly working on, that will detail the significant feats Roosevelt accomplished after the presidency. *The Rise of Theodore Roosevelt* impressed President Reagan so much that he asked Morris to become his official biographer.

If you want to talk about an impressive six-year period in a person's life, look no further than Teddy Roosevelt. When he was 36, he was police commissioner of New York City. When he was 37, he was assistant secretary of the United States Navy. When he was 38, he led the Rough Riders up San Juan Hill in the Spanish-American War. When he was 40, he was elected governor of New York. When he was 42, he was elected vice president of the United States. Later that year, following the assassination of President McKinley, Teddy Roosevelt became the youngest president in our country's history.

Not a bad six-year period, huh? I've gone nearly three months without receiving a parking ticket, and I feel pretty proud of myself. Needless to say, T. R. was in a class all by himself.

What impressed me about this book was how Morris described Roosevelt's early life. He was a sickly child who spent a lot of his youth reading and writing. He actually wrote a field guide to birds that he showcased at the Smithsonian at age 12. T. R. was a speed reader with a photographic memory and could read in six languages. What most impressed me about T. R. was how he was just as comfortable shooting the breeze with cowboys around a campfire as he was discussing Shakespeare with debutantes at a black-tie reception after an evening at the theater.

It is estimated that by the time he was 30, Roosevelt had read over 20,000 books. Yikes! I have to catch up, so I read 10 books a day now. Many of them are scratch-and-sniff and pop-up books, but I honestly read 10 books a day. What I learned from T. R. is that books expand our minds and expose us to new interests. I am a passionate student of the world now because I constantly read about a variety of different things.

For Reflection

Do you agree that aliteracy is as big a problem as illiteracy? What strategies have you used to get students to read? Think of three books that have changed your life, and consider how they did so. What are some ways that you can increase the time that students spend reading in your classroom?

Chapter 7

Some Days Never End

My typical day as a public-school teacher was a lot like my first visit to a horse racing track. It began with anticipation and ended with the realization that this is not the most ideal of settings (the first track I went to reminded me of a bus station, a bowling alley, and downtown Tijuana, all rolled into one).

It's funny—when I first became a teacher, I made a vow to God. "Dear Lord," I said. "I am turning over a new leaf. I am giving up alcohol, and I will never raise my voice or curse again." After my first day of teaching, one of my housemates caught me alone in my room staring at a blank wall, drinking a beer, and shouting obscenities at no one in particular. It's tough being a teacher. Friends used to tell me that I had it easy because teachers only work 180 days a year. I set them straight by pointing out that teachers may only work 180 days a year, but it's hard time.

I started teaching when I was 22. Three years later, I had aged well into my forties. I had a spot of gray hair colleagues called my "ghetto gray." They say a day lasts only 24 hours, but I felt like some of my teaching days dragged on for 50 to 60 hours. One of the most important things I learned through teaching was to look for the little things that would inspire me to fulfill my "perfect day."

I began to wonder what my perfect day would look like, and I realized that little things, not big things, are what matter most. By focusing on the little things I could control, I began to enjoy myself much more in the classroom. What would my perfect day at school look like? I created my own credo to teach by, making sure every day to: (1) play with the kids; (2) enjoy a meal or snack with my colleagues; (3) read the newspaper and something inspirational or funny; (4) sing and dance; (5) write; (6) draw pictures with the kids; (7) teach at least one outstanding lesson; (8) watch a movie clip or listen to a great piece of music; and (9) tell my students I care about them.

I had days when I would go into work feeling great, and at least three of my colleagues would say I looked ill. By the third negative comment, I'd actually feel sick. Think of a time, though, when someone admired your outfit, complimented your appearance, or told you what a great job you do as a teacher. You need to do the same for your kids. Be an Obi-Wan Kenobi rather than a Darth Vader. Once I realized that it does not take much to brighten most people's days, I began making an effort to make every day at school a masterpiece rather than a chore.

It all begins with energy, so I tried to play with my students as much as possible. Feed your brain and your soul with some exercise. When I traveled in China, I was amazed to see that everyone was up at the crack of dawn playing badminton or practicing Tai Chi. So, I would lead my students in stretches, and we'd all recite positive chants to get us pumped for the day.

You need to know something about me, though: I am a highly competitive teacher. I did not become a teacher to be good; I wanted the school renamed after me. I wanted a statue in my honor. I wanted ballads written of my incredible techniques and triumphs. My goal was for students from every other classroom to be pressing their noses against my windows and begging to get into my classroom. I considered every day an opportunity to change the world for the better, and the energy I expounded almost killed me. I set incredibly high standards for my students and myself, and I took it hard whenever we failed to meet those expectations. Rather than focus on the 31 students who accomplished a goal, I beat myself up over the two who failed.

On YouTube, I watched Apple founder Steve Jobs deliver a 2005 commencement address to graduating students at Stanford. During his address, Jobs recited the following adage: "If you live each day as if it was your last," the motto went, "someday you'll most certainly be right." Since then, Jobs looks in the mirror every day and asks, "If today were the last day of my life, would I want to do what I am about to do today?" And whenever the answer has been no for too many days in a row, he knows he has to change something.

That's the way I thought about teaching. Every day was a new experience, and I had to remind myself that I teach because I love learning. Students also need to embrace all the learning opportunities around them.

On the day of his graduation from a little country grade school in Centerton, Indiana, legendary UCLA basketball coach and Hall of Famer John Wooden received a handwritten list from his father with the following useful tips:

1. Be true to yourself.
2. Make each day your masterpiece.
3. Help others.
4. Drink deeply from good books.
5. Make friendship a fine art.
6. Build shelter against a rainy day.
7. Give thanks for your blessings every day.

Before I was married, I tended to drive like a maniac, so I spent many weekends stuck in traffic school. Traffic school is truly one of the best cultural experiences in Los Angeles. It provides a forum for people from many different backgrounds to sit in the same room together for eight hours. One Saturday, I sat between an unforgettable duo. To my left sat a brain surgeon from Long Beach. He was probably six foot five, wore a three-piece suit, and had the most perfect jaw I have ever seen on someone not an anchorman. To my right sat a gangster who had just served 20 years at the state penitentiary. He wore a baggy undershirt and pants, sported a shaved head and tiny moustache, and had tattoos on just about every exposed square inch of his body. I quickly judged both of these gentlemen. By the end of the day, however, I discovered that the ex-convict (someone I had initially judged as menacing and uneducated) was the smartest human being I have ever met (besides my wife).

The traffic-school teacher asked us to state our biggest pet peeve about other drivers. One lady complained about people who fail to signal before changing lanes. A guy in the front row barked about how much he hated people who fail to come to a complete stop at stop signs. Then came time for the ex-convict beside me to speak.

"What bugs you about other drivers?" the teacher asked.

"Nothing," the ex-con replied.

"Come on, there has to be something," the teacher said, and others in the class encouraged the ex-con to share.

"Nothing, man," he said. "There ain't nothing nobody does that I haven't done before."

I realized right then that I have no right to judge anybody, and I can learn from everybody. At the end of each school day, I tried to keep a journal of what worked and what needed improvement. I also kept a journal of funny things the students had done during the day to remind me why I taught. It was one more way to retain my sanity.

Tales from My Classroom

Teaching elementary school with a gang of veterans whose experience far exceeded my own, I soon realized that I broke about 15 to 20 rules during the course of a single day during my first week of teaching. I wrote in my journal about one such experience that involved a boy named Paco:

Paco was a chubby child who had spent the majority of the first day of school picking at a scab the size of a tennis ball on his left forearm. He finally achieved success after lunchtime. He began to bleed, which sparked his wailing, followed by a snorting that eventually turned into an epileptic fit of coughing. Thus, in a brief matter of minutes, Paco had successfully gained the attention of everyone in the class and halted any potential learning of numerators and denominators. Oh well, I thought. It's only math. They can learn fractions next year.

To a seven-year-old, bleeding is much more interesting than reducing two-fourths to a half.

"Mister Brassell," Veronica said in her longest whine of the afternoon. "Paco needs a Band-Aid."

Several heads nodded in unison. My class had found solidarity for the first time all day. Every little move I made that day would be scrutinized and exploited by these young, conniving darlings. The first day had been a game for them to observe my strengths and weaknesses. So far, they were winning. What they did not know, however, was that I knew a thing or two about Band-Aids.

My mother came from a large family that did not have much money, so she was always telling my siblings and me about how good we had it and how bad she had had it. She practically delighted in retelling foreboding anecdotes. Of course, my mom lectured my brother, sister, and me about not picking our scabs. "Scab picking may cause an infection," she'd tell us. "And before you know it, you're dead." Horrific images of death by scab picking haunted my childhood dreams.

Now I looked at Paco and formed a twisted grin on my face. Paco was about to meet my mother.

"I...need...a...Band-Aid," Paco said in between uncontrollable sobs and an occasional cough that sounded just a tad less catastrophic than the eruption of Mount Kilauea. "Cut...hurt...real...bad."

I examined the arm and nodded my head grimly. "That looks serious," I said and looked at the rest of the class. I took a deep breath as if I were the Chief Justice of the Supreme Court handing down a groundbreaking verdict: "Looks like you picked a scab, Paco." He nodded. Guilty, he acknowledged, but ready to receive treatment. I nodded slowly and touched my chin with my right index finger as I stood up.

"Do you know what can happen to you when you pick your scabs?"

Paco shook his head. Just give me my Band-Aid and let me show it to my friends, he was thinking. I looked at Paco and then to the rest of the class, nodding my index finger authoritatively in the air.

"You can get an infection and die."

This did not have the effect I had anticipated. A couple of boys smiled, and Tyrone even giggled. Paco was playing me for a fool in the minds of my fresh batch of second graders. Who does this grown-up think he's fooling?

"I can fix that, though."

"With a Band-Aid," Paco said and grinned. I nodded.

I took Paco by the hand, and we began to walk to my desk. All around us, 32 sets of eyes focused on me with an intensity and concentration normally reserved for presents placed under the Christmas tree. Everyone wanted to see what type of Band-Aid he was going to receive. Many children gasped as if they were witnessing a friend win the lottery, while others smiled and began scratching their arms and licking their lips in hopes of creating their own bloodbaths.

You see, Band-Aids are important to children. In fact, they afford the same status as luxury cars or designer clothes for many adults. Kids are absolutely fascinated by sticky things on their bodies. They love the sensation of peeling something off their skin and reapplying it. Regular stickers are gold. Scratch-and-sniff stickers are platinum. Removable tattoos prompt kids to roll up their sleeves and proudly display their allegiance to Bugs Bunny or Daffy Duck. A Band-Aid tops them all because it is sticky and it exhibits its bearer's ability to endure pain. Not only does a Band-Aid reveal a child's strength—its stickiness usually lasts two to three days longer than other stickers. One's popularity on the playground, therefore, is often directly related to the gluey things clinging to one's body.

No, Paco was not looking for a remedy to his injury. He was seeking a higher social status. A Band-Aid would act as his seal of approval in the playground underworld, and hordes of his comrades would soon be coming to me in search of the same distinction if I was not careful.

Ah, but there's a price to pay for success. This would be one of the only lessons to stick with my students after that first week, but it was a starting point. Paco walked with me back to my desk while the rest of the room eagerly watched. I decided to take my time and turn this into a bigger production than *West Side Story*.

"Hold your horses, Paco," I said. "You'll get better. I'll make sure of it. What you need is a Band-Aid, and you know what?" Paco shook his head. "I don't think any old Band-Aid will do for a cut like yours. I think what you need is a Mighty Morphin Power Ranger Band-Aid!"

Was there an earthquake, or did the room just seem to rock from jaws dropping to the floor? Paco was their hero—the envy of every child in Room 12. A Mighty Morphin Power Ranger Band-Aid! Was this new teacher crazy? That was like gold, silver, and bronze. I could feel the oxygen being sucked out of the classroom as students gasped in disbelief. This new guy is a pushover, they were thinking. Everything I was doing that first week was establishing a precedent, and I was going to make the most of this one.

I opened my "magical medical drawer" and grabbed a Band-Aid. Then I held the sacred bandage in the air for all to admire. Not only was it a Mighty Morphin Power Ranger Band-Aid, but it also featured the Green Ranger, the coolest Power Ranger of them all. Paco's biggest difficulty wasn't masking his pain—it was masking his glee. When word got out that I gave out Mighty Morphin Power Ranger Band-Aids to the wounded, my classroom would become a more popular first-aid station than the nurse's office.

Little eyes focused on the magical medical drawer. It was in the lower left-hand corner of my desk. There was no lock on it, and I made sure never to open it for more than a brief moment. Curiosity and fascination overwhelmed my students as they dreamed of a Band-Aid treasure chest stashed away in my desk. Paco's eyes clouded over as if he had just discovered a gold mine, and others laughed as if all their troubles in life had faded into a distant memory.

I suddenly broke their trance. "Before I put on a Band-Aid," I said, slowly articulating each and every syllable. "I need to clean out the germs in your wound, Paco."

Some students raised eyebrows while others scratched their heads. Suddenly, students were not laughing. They were focusing on something else I was grabbing from the drawer. There was absolute silence.

My hand withdrew from the drawer with two new items. I now held a bottle of clear liquid in my left hand and a cotton swab in my right. Suddenly, the look of adulation on Paco's face turned to one of apprehension. The rest of the class now looked confused.

"You may want to squeeze my arm, Paco," I said. "This stuff can hurt."

Before Paco could argue, I doused the swab with the clear liquid. "Rubbing alcohol," the bottle's label read. I applied it directly to Paco's wound. All of a sudden, Paco screamed with the force of a fire alarm. The other students' eyes filled with horror as they saw their fellow classmate grimace in pain.

Room 12's pupils were no longer smiling. Room 12's pupils were no longer laughing. Room 12's pupils were breathing quickly as if they had just finished wind sprints. Their dreams of limitless Band-Aids had been shattered, and now they looked at their teacher differently. Their eyes did not show respect as much as a new willingness to pay attention. For the first time all day, I could sense their attention.

I placed the Band-Aid over Paco's cut and told him he could lie down if he felt weak. Paco just shook his head, sniffled, wiped his eyes, and rushed to his seat. I looked at the rest of the class and was pleased by their gaping mouths and silent screams of terror. Paco put his head down on his desk while I held the rubbing alcohol in the air. "If anybody else needs a Band-Aid, make sure to ask."

Wide-eyed students began to whisper and glance at the sobbing Paco. They pointed to the medical drawer as if it were the home of a pit bull.

Yes, their looks of joy had dissipated into gasps of fear. When I asked if everyone was ready to continue learning how to create fractions, the students quickly began to copy problems from the chalkboard onto their papers. It was math time in Room 12. There were no more distractions. Students were here to learn.

The tale of the evil medical drawer quickly spread from classroom to classroom. And from that point forward, students in my class—and any other student in the school, for that matter—would rather sit in pain than ask for a Band-Aid from Mr. Brassell.

Note: I soon learned that it was illegal for me to administer any first aid to a student, so I gladly sent my students to the nurse's office (every other Tuesday, when we had a nurse on campus). By the way, Paco was fine and made a full recovery. I, however, received a negative note in my file from the principal, which was to become a daily occurrence.

For Reflection

How did this chapter help you? Think of some of your most vivid memories from the classroom. Consider keeping a journal of your experiences. What other things might you do to help you through the toughest days?

Chapter
8

Flexibility + Perseverance = Results

I love my job. I train beginning teachers and student teachers at California State University, Dominguez Hills. My students will become teachers and school leaders for the next 30 to 40 years. I also get to speak to groups of teachers, parents, administrators, and businesspeople across the United States on the importance of providing quality instruction to students of all ages.

I have had the opportunity to observe thousands of teachers who work with students of all ages in different settings and with different challenges. If I had been given the opportunity to watch so many teachers before I became one, I am convinced that I would have been a better classroom teacher. When people ask me what makes a great teacher, I usually point out that different teachers have different styles, and I can observe 10 great teachers and view their strengths in completely different terms. Based on my observations, though, great teachers have two inherent qualities: they can adapt to anything, and they never give up.

Mario Andretti said, "If things seem under control, you're just not going fast enough." To me, a good classroom is a chaotic classroom. I like to see things moving, and I like a loud room where students are talking and laughing. I know other teachers who keep the volume barely audible and discourage movement. Great teachers, though, seem to have the ability to roll with the punches. You can throw them any curveball, and they will figure out a solution on the spot. And great teachers find a way to teach anyone anything without giving up.

Have you ever had a favorite student? I know you're not supposed to have favorites, but I had a favorite student. When I taught third grade, I had a little boy named Howard. Howard was the son of a Baptist minister, and Howard's father spoke like Martin Luther King Jr., which meant Howard spoke like Martin Luther King Jr.

Whenever I finish a book, I always ask students to applaud the author. On the day we finished reading *Stuart Little*, the kids were all clapping away when a little boy giggled and uttered, "I like Stuart because he's little." This comment prompted Howard to stand.

"Don't you get it?" Howard entoned, his voice steadily rising as he enunciated every syllable. "Don't you get it? We all be little." He paused for effect before shouting. "We all be little! But we be big some day, like Mr. B.," he concluded, pointing at me. It was then that I realized that this child could lead a revolution.

Howard represented the reason I became a teacher. I loved and cherished his unbridled enthusiasm. He put a smile on my face every single day. But I worried for Howard because the following year, he was going to get Ms. Hampton for a teacher. Ms. Hampton was going to misinterpret Howard's enthusiasm as a discipline problem because Ms. Hampton was a direct descendant of Satan.

That was an important lesson for me to learn. If Howard was going to survive fourth grade, he would need to learn to adapt and persevere. All of us are going to have to deal with a Ms. Hampton in our lives sooner or later, and our job as teachers is not to provide students with simple answers. Giving Howard an answer is not going to help him. Our job is to provide students with strategies to be flexible and tenacious—to learn how to deal with the Ms. Hamptons of the world for themselves. These are lifelong skills—skills that teachers especially need to succeed.

Another favorite was Jonathan. Jonathan was one of my most brilliant students. Bright, polite, with a real hunger for knowledge, Jonathan belonged in a gifted program. I had a parent conference with his mother one day and told her how impressed I was by her son.

Jonathan's mother was my idol. She was a single mother working three jobs and raising two of the finest children at our school (his older sister was also brilliant). Jonathan's mother asked me a direct question at our conference that day, and I will never forget it. Most parents just went through the motions during parent-teacher conferences (if they showed up at all), and most assumed I knew what I was doing. You could see on her face that Jonathan's mother worked hard to ensure that her children had a better future, and I took this woman very seriously.

"Mr. Brassell," she said. "Jonathan looks at you like a father. If you were his daddy, what would you do?"

"Move," I heard myself saying without even thinking. "Get him in this other school district where they have a gifted and talented program."

My district did not offer the type of stimulating program that a boy like Jonathan could best benefit from, and I knew that if he stayed at my school, he would have Ms. Hampton next year. I knew Ms. Hampton had a way of draining students' enthusiasm for school right out of their bodies. I did not say this to Jonathan's mother, but that is precisely what I was thinking.

And I knew, then and there, that if that was what I truly believed, then I had to submit my resignation. I submitted it that day. I wound up teaching for the rest of the year, but that was my last year as a full-time teacher. At the time I felt like a failure. I settled into a deep depression after leaving teaching, and it took my mother to lift me out of the doldrums. My mother is a peppy person, and she gave me the pep talk I needed.

"Don't you see, Danny?" she said. "Now your job is to motivate other teachers so that they don't leave teaching. You're going to affect so many more kids this way!"

And that is why I do what I do. I take my job very seriously. You need to know how important you are. We need you, and we value everything you do. Don't ever forget how important you are. Hold your head up and say, "I'm proud to be a teacher." You will not have any control over the Ms. Hamptons or other obstacles that your students will have to face. But if you are flexible enough to adapt to any situation, and are determined to persevere through rough and trying times, you will give your students the strength and confidence they need to thrive.

Teachers are a special breed. I'll never forget teaching summer school. Mrs. Truesdale, the principal who could brag that she had been at this particular school since they laid the foundation (sometime during the Lincoln administration), gave all the teachers a tour of the campus. The first thing she told us was not to expect our paychecks for another three months. We all nodded and moved on. Then she pointed to a chain-link fence with a hole dug under it and said, "Now, make sure you teachers don't let the kids play over here. A pit bull got through there a couple of weeks ago and bit off a kid's nose."

The other teachers and I just nodded and continued walking. Mrs. Truesdale showed us the shades over the windows of some classrooms. "Now, make sure you teachers over here always keep your blinds shut because of drive-by shootings."

Don't open the blinds, I told myself and nodded. Then the principal pointed to a bathroom. "Now, you teachers, don't let the kids go to the bathroom alone because a little first grader got beat up by some fifth graders last month." Send kids in pairs. We all just nodded.

I began to look at my colleagues differently. Are you listening to the horrific things this principal described? I needed serious help, and that is when I discovered the importance of motivation. That will be the topic of Chapter 9. But successful teachers are those who remain flexible through all that is thrown their way and who are determined never to give up.

More Tales from My Classroom

Everything was new to me as a first-year teacher. I kept a record of my experiences in a journal, which served as an outlet for all my trials and tribulations. Here is a story I wrote about one of my little second graders, Belinda:

On the first day of school, Belinda stuck a pencil in Rory's eye and called him a name not suitable to be heard by most adults, let alone a classroom full of seven-year-olds. That earned her a place in time-out.

"Time-out is like jail, Mister Brassell," she said, and she would know. She had spent the majority of her day in time-out. "You should call this jail."

Belinda was right. From that time forward, when students misbehaved and ignored their first two warnings, they were sent to an isolated desk in a corner near my desk known as "jail."

My first year of teaching was probably not too different from any other teacher's first year. I drew praise for my enthusiasm and hard work while secretly realizing I hadn't a clue what I was doing. "And the nominees for best actor in a teaching performance are…Danny Brassell, second grade, inner-city school," I kept telling myself. Belinda knew.

"Mister Brassell, you too young to be a teacher," she said on the second day.

We were getting to know each other well. Belinda, like many of my students, had grown up street-smart, with very little appreciation for school and books. She was one of only three African American girls in my predominantly Spanish-speaking class, and she was not too fond of her Latino classmates conversing in Spanish around her. Belinda was easily the smallest person in my class, and in the past, many of her teachers had fallen into the trap of believing she was "too small and precious to hurt anyone." They might as well have thought the same about a bumblebee.

Jail was not working, so I kept Belinda in at recess. I made her wash all the desks and pick up all the garbage from the floor. That'll teach her, I thought to myself. Belinda, though, was smarter than I was. "I like cleaning, Mister Brassell," she said. "Can I do this every day?"

On the third day, I caught Belinda fighting with José. I walked over to their table and asked what the problem was. "She keeps on calling me a bad word," José said, and after I pressed her for the truth, Belinda finally nodded that she had. Being the smart, perfect-resolution-minded new teacher, I asked José to whisper the bad word into my ear.

"She said I'm stupid," he said, and I was relieved to hear that at least Belinda had toned down her language. Baby steps, I told myself. Belinda wrote standards after school while I gave her another lecture on behavior.

"Belinda, no matter what happens today, just remember that tomorrow is a new day," I said. "Make sure you always keep your head up and try your hardest, and you're bound to improve."

The next day I caught her fighting with José again. Exasperated, I shouted across the room and demanded to know why they were fighting. Again, José said that Belinda had called him a bad word.

"Stop calling José stupid, Belinda," I yelled across the room.

"I didn't call him stupid, Mister Brassell," she yelled back. "I called him a (expletive) (expletive)."

That was it. Belinda had finally earned an angry call home to her mother, but Belinda informed me that her mama did not have a phone. She even smiled when she said it. Determined to win this battle, I told Belinda that I would walk her home after school and talk to her mother in person.

And for the first time all week, Belinda became silent. The rest of the day, she just sat still in her chair, eerily still. The calm before the storm, I thought. At any moment, I expected Belinda to smack somebody next to her or throw something across the room, but she just sat in a trance.

"It's not going to work, young lady," I told her. "You already earned a walk home, and behaving now isn't going to change that."

Belinda just sat quietly, even while the kids around her teased her. For the first time since I met her, Belinda was just a cute little girl sitting subdued in her seat. I could not help but feel a bit of sympathy for her, but I had been told that the only way I would survive as a teacher was to stand firmly by my decisions. So I simply ignored her droopy eyes and frowning lips.

When the final bell sounded, Belinda made a dash for the door, but I reminded her of our appointment. Her shoulders slumped in defeat. She gathered her things, I took her by the hand, and we began the arduous two-block journey to her house. Along the way, it seemed like the entire neighborhood knew Belinda, and this did not appear to be the first time they had seen a teacher walking home with her.

"You in trouble, Belinda?" an old man yelled from his lawn chair on a porch.

Belinda dropped her head.

"Oh, Belinda," said a woman nursing a baby and trying to hold onto two other little ones by her side. "Your mama's gonna whup your behind."

That remark got to me almost as much as it got to Belinda. She just continued to lead me along the sidewalk with her face focused on any weeds or cracks disrupting the surface. Meanwhile, I was nervous as could be. "What kind of teacher am I?" I thought. Here I was, only four days into the school year, and I had lost control of a three-and-a-half-foot seven-year-old. What on earth was I going to say to her mother?

I was trying to reassure myself that I was doing the right thing when Belinda led me through the gate into her yard, which looked more like a trash heap. The bark of a dog the size of a big rig could be heard from inside the house. I let Belinda go inside to get her mother while I waited on the porch. Curious onlookers watched me as if I were an alien who had just landed in a spaceship. I politely smiled, nodded, and waved before focusing again on Belinda's front door like a struggling insurance salesman.

"Where the hell you been, girl?" an angry voice screamed. Babies began crying loudly inside the house.

"My teacher's here," Belinda said softly, and I still could not see inside through the heavily barred front door.

There I stood on the doorstep feeling totally helpless and uncomfortable. What was I doing here? I was treading in uncharted waters and had no idea how to handle this situation. I still wanted to stick to my plan, though, and show Belinda that I meant business.

"Hello," I heard a burly voice say from behind the door, and it sounded more like a "What do you want?" than a salutation. I could barely make out the outline of a disfigured shadow behind the door.

"Uh, I'm Mr. Brassell, Belinda's teacher."

"What'd she do this time?"

All I could envision in my head was a picture of Belinda getting a "whupping." I had actually visualized this with some satisfaction before, thinking a spanking could do Belinda some good. Hearing the anger in her mother's voice, though, I feared Belinda might be in for more than the fanny whacks my father had delivered to me when I misbehaved as a boy. Could I bear to be responsible for Belinda's whupping?

"Well," I stumbled. "I did not come to tell you what Belinda is doing wrong. I came to tell you what she is doing right." There was no response from behind the door, so I continued.

"Belinda really likes to participate in class," I said, searching for whatever true, positive comments I could find for Belinda. Still no response.

"Belinda is also always at school on time, and I wanted to thank you for that," I said. "I really appreciate your support."

The door opened, and a rather skinny, short woman smiled at me. She was in her thirties but looked like she was in her fifties and had scars all over her arms and face. I could finally catch a glimpse of the inside of the cramped little house's floor decor: used 40-ounce malt liquor bottles, crumpled newspapers, and fresh "doggie deposits."

The most unique odor invaded my nostrils, and for the first time since I had been on the porch, the barking and crying subsided.

"I'm Ms. Johnson," she said, offering me her hand to shake. She was practically blushing as she began fidgeting with the curlers in her hair.

She apologized for not inviting me to come inside. My unannounced visit had caught her on a "cleaning day." I smiled and tried to ignore the stench of liquor on Ms. Johnson's breath. I simply stood in her doorway and described every positive thing that Belinda had done over the past week—from sitting quietly as she did her independent work to helping clean the room. I failed to mention that Belinda only sat quietly when I put her alone in "jail" or that she cleaned the room during recess as punishment for bad behavior. It seemed to me that Ms. Johnson had heard those stories about her daughter too many times in the past.

"Well," I concluded, "it was really nice to meet you, Ms. Johnson, and I hope you feel free to come visit our classroom anytime." Now it was Ms. Johnson standing uncomfortably in the doorway with the neighbors staring at her.

"My Belinda's helping other students in her class," I could hear Ms. Johnson yell to an old lady next door as I walked away. "Her teacher says she's really improving."

The next day at school, Belinda gave my knees a big hug. "My mama bought me a new backpack," she said with a smile bigger than her tiny face could hold. "And she said she'd get me a new dolly if I get good grades in your class."

"Are you going to try harder to get along with other people in here?" I asked.

"Yes, sir," Belinda said, and she continued to hug my knees. "You the best teacher."

That made me smile. I had completed my first week of teaching, and despite all the questions I had, one positive comment from one little seven-year-old provided all the motivation in the world to me.

This was what I would come to know as the inner-city teaching experience.

For Reflection

Think about your most challenging students, and your most rewarding students. Perhaps they are the same group. What is it about them that makes your job interesting? How do you draw motivation and inspiration from such students? Think of one action item related to flexibility and one related to perseverance that you gained from this chapter.

Motivation

I have learned that I cannot motivate another human being. I can only inspire them to motivate themselves. Long-lasting motivation comes from within, but sometimes we need others to give us a little nudge in the right direction.

Chapter 9

Seek Out a Mrs. Turner

I taught in a school district with very few white teachers, where I was one of the few men teaching young children. Most of the teachers I worked with were older African American women from the South who had been teaching for 30 years or more.

Mrs. Turner was my mentor teacher. As far as I am concerned, her picture should be on a stamp. She was the guiding light in my darkest days.

She had been teaching for nearly 40 years. She was from Alabama, and she believed in two things: discipline and the Bible. When her little ones got out of line, she had no qualms about taking out her Bible and reading verses from the book of Revelation to her children. Her respect had to be earned, and it took her awhile to decide I was not all that bad.

We were team teachers. That meant our two classes were blessed to get me for part of the day and Mrs. Turner for the other part. What a great experience for them. They were exposed to the tried-and-true traditional teaching methods of a wise African American woman and the energy of a young white guy who did not have a clue what he was doing.

All I ever needed to learn about teaching I learned from Mrs. Turner. She was cross but compassionate, firm yet fair. For years, she spent her Monday mornings before school cleaning up her classroom from the damage of weekend vandals. She wanted her classroom free from the graffiti and violence that was common on the outside. She suffered no fools, and she could spot a scam artist from a mile away. She could detect more than a store surveillance camera, and people who mistook her silence for passivity had another thing coming.

Mrs. Turner gave me my favorite quote about teaching. "Each and every one of my children is gifted," she said. "It just takes some of them a little longer to unwrap the presents." She also made me laugh.

One day I saw her struggling with one of the students, Francisco Hernandez. All of a sudden, I saw Mrs. Turner throw her hands into the air and let out a primal scream of frustration. She tapped her fingers along his paper as if counting and declared, "Child, you have 12 different letters in your name. If you can figure out how to write your name, you'll learn half the alphabet!" I don't know a teacher who has not had a day like that, and it made me feel a little better about my own teaching frustrations to see a colleague lose her mind.

Without Mrs. Turner, I do not know if I could have survived my first year of teaching. She was always there to lend a guiding hand. Like a good football coach, she had that rare ability to know when to scold and when to praise. She did not tolerate people talking down to teachers, and she stuck up for me more than once.

We had a difficult principal at the time. I have had great principals, and I have had horrific principals. If you have a terrific principal, make sure to praise him or her every chance you get because great principals are worth their weight in platinum. I have had some mighty poor principals who have led me to question where districts find some of these people.

I know God has a sense of humor because I used to pray for a new principal. "Dear Lord," I'd say, "Please find us a new principal. There cannot be anybody worse than this person."

Amazingly, I found out, there can be. We had a principal that I will call Mrs. Lucifer. She was a nightmare. She was replaced by Voldemort. He was a nightmare, a jerk, and an idiot all rolled into one. I'm not sure how he had ever become an administrator, but my bet is that he won the position in a card game.

Mrs. Turner dealt with him by completely blowing him off. At every faculty meeting, she took out her Mary Higgins Clark novel and read. Whenever she was addressed, she'd agree with Voldemort and duck her head right back behind her novel. Union guidelines said that meetings could only last until 3:30 P.M. At 3:31 P.M., Mrs. Turner would rise, point to her watch, and announce, "Somebody needs a timekeeper." Then she'd walk right out of the meeting, much to the chagrin of Voldemort and the delight of all nontenured faculty.

I have never wanted to punch someone as much as I wanted to punch this principal. He was a bully who prided himself on putting teachers and students down. Before I could get myself in trouble for decking him, Mrs. Turner took me aside and advised me on how to deal with menacing administrators.

"Mr. Brassell," she said. "The next time someone like that comes into your room, just do as I do: Say 'uh-huh' and nod your head. Say 'uh-huh' and nod your head again. Then say 'oh!' and point your finger in the air and open your eyes wide as if you just heard something never before suggested by humankind. Then shut your door and teach your class your way. I've been teaching at this school for over 40 years, and they've had 35 different reading programs. I've got one—mine—and it works."

They don't make them like Mrs. Turner anymore.

The irony is that despite all my run-ins with administrators, I eventually became an administrator. In defense of administrators, I have this to say: If you think there's pressure on teachers, administrators have it tenfold. There is nothing but pressure on administrators to raise test scores. Nearly a quarter of all school administrators in the United States are in their first year on the job. Try to cut them some slack.

But never miss a chance to find a mentor like Mrs. Turner.

Wisdom from My Mentor

Mrs. Turner was my mentor, and she is one of the greatest people I have ever known. She provided me with quirky tidbits of advice that almost always saved me from pulling the remaining strands of hair from the top of my head.

1. Bring a broom on Monday morning.

Mrs. Turner's classroom and mine were vandalized on a weekly basis. While I fretted and complained, Mrs. Turner silently took out a broom every Monday morning and cleaned up the mess. She taught me to keep my mouth shut and deal with curveballs. "We're in the business of putting out fires and cleaning up other people's messes," she'd say. "Our little ones are going to bring baggage to the classroom, and we've got to figure out how to make room for it and get some teaching done."

2. Pray.

I never could have been a teacher without the support of Mrs. Turner and the other great women that I taught beside. Mrs. Turner was a deeply religious woman, so she gathered all the teachers from our grade level together in her classroom at the end of the day to lead us in prayer. Now, some of what she said made me laugh, and I cannot mention some of the things she prayed for in our circle. What I can say is that Mrs. Turner's prayer circles brought me closer to my colleagues and taught me a lesson in seeking and providing support. Effective teaching should not be a lonely business; there is no shame in obtaining guidance and expertise.

3. If you're not funny, don't crack jokes.

Mrs. Turner had no illusions about what her strengths and weaknesses were as a teacher. She was quite comfortable playing the role of a disciplinarian who was all about getting things done. Whenever I strayed from my own strengths, Mrs. Turner reminded me that every teacher brings his or her own style. The only non-negotiables are love and patience for your students.

4. Bring a sack lunch.

I can probably count on one hand how many times I ever

managed to go off-campus for lunch during my lunch period. I rarely even made it to the teacher's lounge (that is, once we had a teacher's lounge). My sack lunch was more like a sack brunch, because it was largely consumed during morning and afternoon recess breaks. I, like most teachers, tended to have little time at lunch to actually eat. That was my time to talk with parents, make phone calls, and manage discipline problems.

5. Work will always be there—keep it there.

Mrs. Turner noticed that I always arrived earlier and left later than everyone else at school, and she could see it was taking its toll. She took me by the arm one day and asked me if I had a girlfriend. "No," I stuttered, wondering where she was headed with this line of inquiry. "Well, you better go get one," she said. "Work will always be there, no matter how much you do. So let go." That was a great tip, and I made sure to keep a saner schedule. Because of it, my time at school actually became more productive.

6. See the beauty in your students.

Despite her thick shell, Mrs. Turner was a gentle soul. Occasionally, I caught her smiling about something a child had said or done, and she was the one who recommended I purchase a journal to keep track of funny things my students said. "Remind yourself why you became a teacher," she would tell me.

7. Don't confuse mandates with teaching.

The most important thing I learned from Mrs. Turner was that I became a teacher to teach kids, not appease administrators or parents. "As long as you focus on the children," she said, "you can never go wrong."

For Reflection

How did you benefit from this chapter? Reflect on the relationships you've had, either as a mentor or a mentee. If you are an experienced teacher, is there a younger teacher who might profit from such a relationship with you? If you are a younger teacher, is there someone in your school you would like to have as a mentor?

Chapter 10

Your Attitude Makes or Breaks You

Keith Harrell says that your attitude is everything, and I completely agree. How you think affects how you behave.

Are you a Tigger or an Eeyore? I am a Tigger, and my wife is an Eeyore. I typically come home bouncing and ask my wife how her day was. She'll shrug as if to say, "Thanks for noticing me." I am curious to see how our children will turn out.

I am seriously hyperactive. When I was a kid, it was called curiosity and enthusiasm. Nowadays, they prescribe medication for it. I used to ask my colleagues why I had so many hyperactive students. I'd pose this question as I tapped a leg, shook my head, and gnawed on a pen. Attitude, like my hyperactive energy, is contagious. Your students will reflect your behavior and your attitude.

Speaker and author Wayne Dyer says that when you change the way you look at things, the things you look at change. He's right. To paraphrase Henry Ford: Whether you believe you can do a thing or not, you are right. Put more directly, if you think your students will succeed, they will succeed. And if you believe they are not capable of success, they will fail.

Your attitude is everything. You have to make sure you are in a positive state of mind, receptive to the great things each school day has to offer. I have learned to always listen to the upbeat radio station on the way to work. My first day of teaching, as I drove into the school's parking lot, the song on the radio was Pink Floyd's "The Wall."

"We don't need no education," they sang, and I was freaked out.

You can bet I listened to a different radio station from that point forward to put me in the right mind-set for each school day.

Commit to an attitude of constantly striving for the best within yourself. It's a lesson I learned from Ms. McClain in 11th grade that has stuck with me all these years.

I train student teachers and beginning teachers at the university now, and I give all my students As. When people ask how I get away with that, I always say that the day someone can show me research that indicates a direct relationship between grades received and knowledge acquired, I'll start grading. When I was a student, I took plenty of classes that dragged while I goofed off and did next to nothing, and I received As. I've also taken classes where I worked my butt off and learned a lot, only to earn a C. I tell my university students that if they get a lot out of my class, I will accept half the credit, and if they don't learn a thing, I'll take half the blame. I want to empower my students to learn for the sake of self-growth rather than for a grade. It's all about their attitude.

I typically deal with two types of students at the university. One student approaches me and explains that he or she is interested in taking my class. When he or she asks me how difficult my class is, I ask the student what his or her other classes at the university have been like. If the student says that his or her other classes have been terrible, I put a hand on the student's shoulder, shake my head, and apologize, "Oh! Well, you'll hate this class, then." Another student comes up to me and asks me the same question, and I, in turn, ask about his or her experiences in other university classes. When the student tells me that he or she has had a delightful time and learned a ton in other courses, I grin and confirm, "Well, then, you're going to love this class."

Our thoughts become our reality, and I constantly point out to students the importance of believing in themselves. We were not placed on this planet to fail. Each of us has greatness within ourselves, and our job as teachers is to help students unleash their greatness within.

I love using poetry in my classroom for a number of reasons.

Poems are succinct. They are great to use as icebreakers or transitional activities. Poetry is an excellent form of expression and a great tool for getting students interested in writing. I love exposing students to different poets and their backgrounds.

One of my favorite poets is Emily Dickinson. While she was an amazing poet, I point out to students that Emily Dickinson only published a handful of poems while she was alive. She did not expose her art to the world, and were it not for Emily Dickinson's sister, her poetry would have died with her. It was not until after her death that the world was blessed with Dickinson's work. What a shame that Dickinson, a recluse, never knew the joy her poetry would bring the world. So I ask students, will you die without sharing your poetry, whether it is writing or singing or shooting a basketball or inspiring students to learn? You can do anything you want, but don't leave this world regretting what you could have done.

Love what you do, whatever it is. Cynthia Rylant's poem "When I Was Young in the Mountains" (1993) contains one of my favorite verses for students and teachers alike to remember:

"When I was young in the mountains, I never wanted to go to the ocean, and I never wanted to go to the desert. I never wanted to go anywhere else in the world, for I was in the mountains. And that was always enough."

Take satisfaction and joy in what you do. You are making a positive contribution every day! An optimistic perspective will take you far. Optimistic teachers prevail because they don't give up at the first sign of difficulty. They recognize that some students grasp concepts in 10 minutes, while other students may not get it until April. The important thing for teachers to remember is that all students have amazing potential inside of them. Great teachers believe in their students.

A positive attitude will take you far. I was given a class of Spanish-speaking students and told to teach them how to read and write in Spanish, even though I spoke limited Spanish myself. I could have quit then and there, but instead, I embraced the challenge. I learned

Spanish by working with young, forgiving students and developing strategies to increase my vocabulary as much as possible. My trick was to translate show tunes into Spanish, like the song "Tomorrow" from *Annie*.

"¡Mañana! ¡Mañana! ¡Te amo! ¡Mañana! Solamente un día más," I'd sing.

Don't take yourself too seriously. I laugh at myself every day, and the students laugh at me at least 300 times a day. I mentioned earlier that my favorite student of all time was a third grader by the name of Howard. Howard's favorite song went like this:

"If you're happy and you know it, clap your hands!

If you're happy and you know it, clap your hands!

If you're happy and you know it, do us all a favor— show it (and Howard would grin broadly).

If you're happy and you know it, clap your hands!"

I have four axioms that I'd like you to stand up and read aloud:

1. I refuse to be afraid of enjoying myself in my classroom.
2. My students feel my passion.
3. I do not have to scowl for people to take me seriously.
4. I am excited to be here.

Seven Cool Ways to Affect Attitude

The law of attraction, according to Wayne Dyer, states that you reap what you sow. You are what you think, so think good stuff.

While many things are beyond my control and my students' control, we can control our frames of mind. Sometimes, the only difference between something bad and something good is perspective. Many of the bad things that happen to us turn out to be good things. I emphasize quality of thought with my students, and here are seven cool ways I try to impact my students' attitudes:

1. **Community Call-Outs**

    I watched a video of a second-grade classroom in Japan where the teacher devoted the last 10 minutes of every day for students to rise and praise classmates who helped them throughout the day. It was one of the most beautiful demonstrations of public praise I have ever seen, and I adopted it immediately. You will not believe how much students look forward to being recognized by their peers for good deeds.

2. **Five Pennies**

    I got this idea from a minister in Missouri. Give each of your students, whether they are kindergartners or high school seniors, five pennies. They must begin each day with the pennies in their right pocket, and every time they compliment a classmate they must transfer a penny to their left pocket. The goal is for students to end the day with five pennies in their left pocket. I emphasize to students that I am not here to make them smarter. I am here to make them better. Practicing kindness every day is one of the best ways to improve your attitude and the attitude of the people around you.

3. **A Simple Trick**

    Whenever I encounter a student who is in a foul mood or pouting, I put my two index fingers in the air and threaten to change their frown into a smile with my bare hands. This usually draws laughs (unless the student is a middle school student, and then it draws glares).

Encourage students to watch funny movies and television shows, read silly comic strips or joke books, and listen to positive radio stations. They have the rest of their lives to worry about life. Youth is about possibilities, and I want my students to feel like they can take on anything.

My parents have a photo of me as a child wearing a fireman's helmet, space boots, a football jersey, and a sheriff's badge. What I love about the photo is that it captures, in my eyes, what childhood should be about: dreaming big dreams.

4. Chants

I lead my students in various chants throughout the day to get them pumped up about what we are learning and what we can accomplish. Bring this book to school and say, "Students stand up and repeat after me":

> **"Welcome"**
> This is the class—
> Who wants to learn,
> And read more books,
> And make a better tomorrow!
>
> ---
>
> **"Bienvenidos"**
> ¿Quieres aprender? ¡Sí!
> ¿Quieres aventura? ¡Sí!
> ¿Quieres leer? ¡Sí!
> ¿Qué tienen información? ¡Libros!
> ¿Qué tienen fotos bonitos? ¡Libros!
> ¿Qué tienen cuentos? ¡Libros!

"Let's Get Excited!"

2, 4, 6, 8—
What do we appreciate?
Reading! Reading! Yeah!
Let's have some fun!

"Let's Go!"

Let's go!
Let's go!
L-e-t-s g-o.
Let's
(clap-clap, clap-clap)
Go!
(clap-clap, clap-clap)

"School Rocks!"
(to the tune of the USC fight song)
It's real-ly
Good to be
Here in this class.
Oh, lucky me!
I'm going
To learn so much.
I'll try my best
To work and play.
Oh—don't you see? I'm on my way
To victory
In school!

5. Role Models

Read short inspirational biographies to your students. Students need to hear about other people overcoming obstacles. The reason I love to read biographies aloud to students is to point out to them that no one ever got anywhere without believing in themselves. Their attitudes played a huge role in their successes.

6. Triumph Journals

Encourage students to keep journals that detail all their successes. Teachers need to keep these journals as well. Review them often and pay attention to everything that works for you. People who succeed constantly think about what it takes to succeed.

7. Compliment Sheets

You've probably heard the story before, but it inspires me, so I'll remind you of it. (I do not know if it really happened, but that does not matter because the message of the story is true.) A teacher asked her students to divide a piece of paper into two columns. She told the students to list the names of all their classmates in one column and to write down the nicest thing they could say about each person in the other column. Her students had been quarreling, and she wanted to put an end to all the negative feelings in the room.

Well, the teacher spent the weekend creating individual sheets for each student that listed all the compliments their classmates had written about them. As students read their sheets of compliments the following Monday, silence ensued, and before long, everyone was beaming with pride and joy.

No one ever mentioned those papers in class again. The teacher did not know whether her students ever discussed their compliment sheets with their classmates or parents, but it didn't matter. Students finally began to work well together and respect one another's feelings.

That group of students moved on, and several years later, one of the students was killed in Vietnam. The teacher attended the funeral of her former student. There, the student's father presented the teacher with the flag that had draped his son's casket. She did not understand.

"I want to show you something," the fallen soldier's father said, taking a wallet out of his pocket. "They found this on Mark when he was killed. I thought you might recognize it."

Opening the billfold, he carefully removed a worn piece of paper that had obviously been taped, folded, and refolded many times. The teacher knew, without looking, that the paper was the same one she had listed all the good things each of the soldier's classmates had said about him on that day in fifth grade many years before. At this point, the teacher could barely contain herself and tears streamed down her face. Gradually, a small crowd of her former fifth graders, the soldier's former classmates, gathered around her.

"I still have my list," one man explained. "It's in the top drawer of my desk at home."

"My husband asked me to put his in our wedding album," offered a woman.

"I have mine, too," another man said. "It is hanging on the wall behind the desk in my office."

Finally, another woman reached into her purse, took out her wallet, and showed her teacher the worn and frayed list.

I love that story because it shows how a kind word can go a long way in strengthening a person's attitude.

For Reflection

Think about the tips shared in this chapter. In what ways can you affect your students' attitudes about learning? In what ways can you affect your attitude about teaching? How have you already done this? Has it been effective?

Chapter 11

Have Lots of Tricks Up Your Sleeve (And Don't Show All Your Cards)

President Harry S. Truman said that it is amazing what you can get accomplished when you don't care who gets the credit. In teaching, I have learned to trick students into motivating themselves. The way you do that is by making them think it was their idea. It's a spousal trick I picked up.

When I began teaching, I did not have a lot of money, which meant I did not have a lot of money to spend on incentives for my students. My school did, however, have an ample supply of construction paper, so whenever I caught my students doing something well, I'd give them a "blue buck." A blue buck was a blue piece of construction paper. Once a student earned 10 blue bucks, he could trade those in for a "red square," which was a red piece of construction paper. If a student earned five red squares, he could trade those in for a "green note," which was a green piece of construction paper. And everybody in my classroom knew that earning a green note was a big, big deal.

My students would be out on the playground with students from other classes bragging that they had earned a green note. Students from other classes would look at them, dumbstruck, and say, "That's just a piece of construction paper!" I learned from Ms. Whitt back in eighth grade that students value whatever the teacher values.

When I lead training sessions for secondary teachers, they often remark that those sorts of tricks do not work with older students. Are you kidding me? The middle school and high school students that I have worked with are even easier to trick.

Let's say Niceysha Jackson has been doing well in class. I will hand her a note. "Niceysha, I want you to take this note home to your mother," I say, "and don't read it." What's Niceysha going to do? She's going to read the note. And she is going to realize how awesome she truly is.

> *Dear Ms. Jackson,*
>
> *In all my years of teaching, I have never had a student as brilliant as your daughter. Niceysha is a leader who helps her classmates and always tries her hardest. I am so proud of the example she sets for others, and she is a delight to have in my class. I envision her as a future president or business owner. Thank you so much for your support!*
>
> *Sincerely,*
>
> *Mr. Brassell*
>
> *P.S. Please don't tell Niceysha that I wrote you this letter.*

The next day, Niceysha walks into my classroom with her head held high. She says nothing, but she has an air about her now that says, "The teacher thinks I'm pretty incredible."

It is so easy to get in their little minds. Sometimes I have to switch things up to break up a stale day. For example, students who tattle are one of my biggest pet peeves. I tell students that people tattle for three reasons. First, they want attention. Secondly, they want to get somebody in trouble. Thirdly, someone is in danger. Now, if someone is in danger, I insist that students tell me immediately, but if they are tattling for either of the other two reasons, students know that whatever punishment I issue the student who is tattled on, the tattler gets the exact same punishment.

I handle tattletales in two ways. A colleague gave me a poster of an elderly woman whom the kids and I named Mrs. Fields, after the cookie lady. Whenever a student approached me to tattle for no good reason, I'd say that I did not have time to deal with his or her problem, and I'd send the student over to Mrs. Fields. So the little one would walk over to the poster and start tattling to it. One of my little boys, Sergio, had been talking to Mrs. Fields for nearly 20 minutes one day.

"Is everything all right, Sergio?" I asked.

"Mrs. Fields is working it out for me," he said. Whatever works.

I have found that students are just like all adults. What they really want is the right to gripe. So my second way of handling tattletales is to create a center with a "case docket" book. Whenever students had a problem, based on their level of literacy, they'd write the problem down, draw it, scribble it in Sanskrit—whatever. Once we accomplished our goals for the day, my students have free-choice time. One of the options available to them is called the People's Court.

If students choose the People's Court (and it is one of the most popular activities in our class), I'll ask my student of the day to act as the bailiff and call the court to order.

"All rise and raise your right hand," the bailiff will say. "Do you all swear to tell the truth, the whole truth, and nothing but the truth? If so, say 'I do.'"

After all the students repeat, "I do," the bailiff asks them all to be seated.

"People's Court is now in session. The Honorable Judge Brassell presiding."

"Thank you, Madame Bailiff," I'll say. "Can you please read the first case?"

"Case No. 1," the bailiff reads. "*Omunique v. José.*"

Now things start swinging. It looks like a scene straight out of *Law*

& Order. Omunique is the plaintiff, and José is the defendant, and students are raising hands and begging to cross-examine the witnesses. What I have learned above all else from this activity is that if I am ever on trial, I want none of my students on my jury. That's because my kids only know one word: guilty.

"This court hereby finds the defendant, José, guilty of hitting Omunique," I announce. "But because honesty is the best policy, and José confessed to his offense, I hereby sentence José to apologize to Omunique and give her a hug."

All the kids cheer, and half the time the students made up the argument in the first place so they would have the chance to play the People's Court. Like any good activity, the People's Court is fun, engaging, and covers at least 10 different standards in the curricula (it is worth doing for the oral-language practice alone).

Sometimes I trick the kids to maintain my own sanity. There are plenty of times when students will get bored and become unruly in my class. In those instances, I ask my "aides" for help. "All right, kids, I see you're a little bit excited today," I say. "Since you won't listen to me, I've asked Australian Pete to come read to you." I'll leave the room and wander back in, acting like I just rode a kangaroo in from the outback.

"G'day, mates," I say. "I just got done puttin' a shrimp on the barbie. Your teacher says you want me to read to you." The kids all cheer, excited to see Australian Pete.

By the end of the day, the kids can get quite rowdy. In those cases, I'll invite the grumpy old man to the room. I'll exit and return slowly, hunched and snarling.

"Your teacher says you want me to read to you," I growl. "Be quiet, first!"

The kids giggle and applaud. "We love grumpy old man!"

I've learned to keep my eyes open because inspiration can be found in many places, and tricks are invaluable to teaching.

Some More of My Favorite Tricks

I've always tried to create a fun, student-centered environment that encourages a lot of play and interaction. Here are some more ideas on how to accomplish classroom business without sacrificing silliness:

1. Word Master

Never let them see you sweat. Inevitably, on the first day of school, I will write something on the chalkboard that prompts a student to point out, "Mr. Brassell, you misspelled a word."

"Yes," I say. "This is a game we're going to play all year to see if you're paying attention. From time to time, I will intentionally misspell a word. Now which word is it?"

2. Gifted and Talented

Students will meet your expectations, so set high expectations. I was once assigned the problem students by an administrator who assured me that all I had to do was babysit these students before they found their way to the juvenile detention facility. Folks, if that is the expectation, what chance do these students have? I decided to take a different approach.

"I've never taught in the gifted and talented program before," I announced to the students on the first day. "You guys are really going to have to help me out."

The students looked at one another with raised eyebrows. "Doesn't this guy know who we are?" they asked one another. I did not find out until two days before the end of the school year that all my students had folders chronicling their educational histories. The truth is, I am glad I didn't have that information because most of it was negative. The less I know about a student, the better (in most cases). I told students they all had clean slates with me, and it is amazing how much you can accomplish when you believe it is possible.

3. Phone Call Roulette

One of my biggest pet peeves is when students fail to communicate to their parents what they are learning in school. To prevent that, I used to make seven random phone calls each night (I had 33 students, so seven calls a night over a five-day work week could cover the entire class) to ask parents what goals we accomplished in class that day. If the parent could name three to five goals we had accomplished, that student would earn a sticker for his or her group. It only took a couple of weeks before every parent knew what we were doing in class.

4. Lunch Line "Shakes"

At least one teacher had to supervise students at my school as they waited to get into the cafeteria, which could sometimes take classes up to half an hour. I saw no sense in all my colleagues wasting their lunch breaks, so I usually volunteered to wait with all the students. When a couple hundred hungry kids are standing around with nothing to do, trouble is just around the corner. I used to distract the kids by leading them in songs. Their favorite was to the beat of KC and the Sunshine Band's "Shake, Shake, Shake."

"Shake, shake, shake," we sang as we wiggled our fingers. "Shake, shake, shake. Shake your fingers. Shake your fingers."

"Shake, shake, shake," we sang as we put a finger on our noses. "Shake, shake, shake. Shake your nose. Shake your nose."

The kids always anticipated the big finale as we began to twist our hips. "Shake, shake, shake. Shake, shake, shake. Shake your booty! Shake your booty!"

I hated missing lunch most days, but some of my fondest memories consist of leading a couple hundred kids in "shaking their booties."

5. Lineups

My students and I always got a kick out of lining up for lunch and recess. Sometimes I would dismiss students from their seats by asking them to solve math problems. Other times I would have them line up if they could answer questions about state capitals or U. S. presidents. Their favorite, however, was when I would dance around the room to the beat of Queen's "Another One Bites the Dust."

"Duh, duh, duh," I'd say as I tapped a student on the head for them to get in the lunch line. "Another one goes to lunch. Duh, duh, duh. Another one goes to lunch. And another one does, and another one does. Another one goes to lunch. Oh! He's gonna get you, too. Another one goes to lunch!"

6. Ask Three Before Me

Don't you hate it when you give students directions, ask if there are any questions, and no one says a thing? Then, once you tell students to begin, one student immediately asks you what to do? I handle that in two ways.

First, I set a timer. Students are not allowed to ask me anything for five minutes. This encourages them to ask questions when I ask them to or to seek help from their classmates. Secondly, I insist that students ask three of their classmates for assistance before they ever come to me. I want to teach them to solve problems on their own.

7. Greet Students at the Door

I like to start the day off with positive energy, so I personally greet every student as they enter the classroom. I ask students if we are going to have a good day and try to give them a compliment or tip of the day. I will also give students special challenges, like half of a compound word (they have to match theirs with a classmate), a famous person (they have to match their person with a classmate's description of what that person did), etc.

8. Clipboard Assessment

One of the easiest and most beneficial ways I assess students is through daily observation, so I walk around the room with a clipboard and take general notes about the class and specific notes on approximately seven students' individual index cards (again, I typically had 33 students, so by observing seven per day, I could cover the entire class in the course of a week).

9. Hot Square

Most of my students speak English as a second language, and they often have trouble understanding me. We cover a lot of information, but whenever there is something that I think is particularly important for them to understand, I stand on the "hot square," a red square I have taped to the floor to emphasize important information to students. While many of my colleagues argue that everything they say is important for students to remember, I would argue that most of what we say is really not that important. The action of standing in a special place, though, visually calls out critical information for students to remember.

10. Morning Meeting Broadcasts

If it were up to me, I'd run my entire school day like a morning meeting broadcast. Over the years, I have learned that students learn next to nothing from me; they learn almost everything from one another. Morning meeting broadcasts turn control of the class over to the students, and I love watching students run the classroom routines with little to no assistance from me.

Our morning meetings are similar to other morning meetings, only we format them like a local newscast. There are anchors to report important news, dates, and assignments; a person for the weather and plants report; a person to chronicle sports feats accomplished by the class; and plenty of field reporters to show and tell, review inspirational quotes, report on important events on this day in history, etc. The trick is to let the kids run the show.

For Reflection

Think of two or three new tricks you picked up from this chapter. Is there a fine line where motivation can become counterproductive manipulation? If so, how can you avoid crossing it? What are some of the most effective tricks you've used in your classroom?

Games Are Good

Mary Poppins was right. She was an important educational philosopher in the mid-1960s. She gave us bits of wisdom like "supercalifragilisticexpialidocious" and "A spoonful of sugar helps the medicine go down." She also said something that helped guide my teaching philosophy: "For every job there is to be done, there is an element of fun." Translation: Games are good.

I know a woman who has been teaching for over 40 years who says she has never once assigned homework. She assigns "homegames." Watch me as I knock my forehead with my fist. Why didn't I think of that? She's right. How we phrase things can make all the difference. Make kids think it's a game, and they will choose to do it on their own. I watched this teacher enthusiastically tell her little ones that they were going to get to play the workbook game at home tonight, and the kids jumped out of their seats cheering.

Kids and adults think differently. We could probably solve most of the world's problems if we left them to children to decide. (Some might argue that many of our leaders think like children, but I think this is unfair to children). We could learn so much more if we paid closer attention to our children. They are processing information constantly and viewing problems through fresh lenses.

Spelling can be a nightmare to many students, especially since English has so many contradictory rules. My students and I turned spelling into a game, though. Sometimes we'd write words in the air; other times we'd type words out with our feet. We even hopped on "letter tiles" on the floor to correctly spell different sight words. As a result, my students became excellent spellers who have a passion for spelling words correctly.

One game I play with students is called "Unhook Yourself from Fonics." We begin this game with our fish "hook" and reel in words, beginning with the word *fish*. I'll ask students to spell *fish*, and they will tell me the accepted spelling. Then I challenge students to spell the word in the most phonetic ways possible, even in bizarre phonetic ways. So *fish* could be spelt *phish* or even, and this is my favorite, *ghos*. If you take the /gh/ sound from *enough*, the /o/ sound from *women* and the /s/ sound from *sugar*, the spelling *ghos* can be pronounced like *fish*. The point is to explore the strange and wonderful diversity of spelling in English.

I have learned to always look for additional "right" answers because while I am thinking in a certain way, students often examine questions from a totally different (and refreshing) perspective. For example, when I was in kindergarten, Sister Roseanna asked the class if we all wanted to go to heaven. All of us raised our hands except Hector. Sister Roseanna scolded Hector and accused him of being a nonbeliever.

"You don't want to go to heaven?" she asked in a condescending and accusatory tone.

"Oh," Hector said. "I thought you meant today."

Hector was not trying to be difficult. He just interpreted the question from a different point of view.

I encourage my students to think creatively all the time. I take any problem, turn it into a game, and examine how many different ways we can solve a particular problem. By playing games, we can cover several academic standards related to problem solving and working with others. The activity leads students to look at everything from different points of view.

Games encourage students to think differently. Unfortunately, schools often discourage creativity. In his book *AHA!*, Jordan Ayan writes, "My wife and I went to a (kindergarten) parent-teacher conference and were informed that our budding refrigerator artist, Christopher, would be receiving a grade of 'Unsatisfactory' in art. We were shocked. How could any child—let alone our child—receive a poor grade in art at such a young age? His teacher informed us that he had refused to color within the lines, which was a state requirement for demonstrating 'grade-level motor skills'" (1996).

Gordon MacKenzie's studies of schools in *Orbiting the Giant Hairball* (1998) were even more appalling:

"How many artists are there in the room?" he asked. "Would you please raise your hands?" When MacKenzie posed the question to first graders, the children leapt *en masse* from their seats, arms waving. Every child was an artist. In the second-grade classrooms he visited, about half the kids raised their hands, shoulder high, no higher. The hands were still. In third-grade classrooms, at best, 10 kids out of 30 would raise a hand, tentatively and self-consciously. By the time MacKenzie reached sixth-grade classrooms, he writes, no more than one or two kids raised their hands, and then, ever so slightly, betraying a fear of being identified by the group as a "closet artist."

"The point is," MacKenzie says, "every school I visited was participating in the suppression of creative genius."

Maria Montessori said that "the most favorable time for a child to learn is when she wants to do it herself…Education is not something which the teacher does, but…it is a natural process which develops spontaneously in the human being." I believe that the more your students work, play, and solve problems on their own, the better.

Nearly a Dozen Games to Stimulate and Educate

Contrary to popular belief, games serve very important academic purposes. Games allow students to master new skills and concepts, including number and shape recognition, grouping, and counting; letter recognition and reading; visual perception and color recognition; eye-hand coordination and manual dexterity, etc. Just because you have fun doing something does not mean it is not important. In fact, I have found that students retain much more information when it is presented as a game because students learn best when they are at ease and enjoying meaningful experiences.

Child psychiatrist Alvin Rosenfeld says, "Just by virtue of playing them, board games can teach important social skills such as communicating verbally, sharing, waiting, taking turns, and enjoying interaction with others." Good old-fashioned board games are just one of the many types of games I like to offer my students. Here are some other favorites:

1. **California (or, insert your state) Jones**

   This is a popular center for all ages. The students are archaeologists who discover amazing treasures every day. They just have to figure out what they are. The goal is to come up with as many possible uses for the object as your brain can muster. For example, seeing a staple remover, California Jones might explain that it is a set of alligator jaws, a shoelace-untying device, a weapon, an ear piercer, medieval tweezers, a primitive puppet, or an ice-cube-grabbing device.

2. **One Up, One Down**

   One of my favorite games to play with middle school and high school students is called One Up, One Down. There are only two rules to the game. The first rule is that when it is your turn, you can say one of three things: (1) one up, one down; (2) two up; or (3) two down. The second rule is that you cannot say the same thing on two consecutive turns.

   The secret to the game is that whatever you say has to correspond to where your hands are at that moment (but you do not reveal this to the student volunteers). You, the instructor, begin by saying one of the three phrases and ask the first student volunteer to your right to say one of the phrases. If the student says "two up" and her hands are down, you say, "No!" If the student guesses correctly, praise that student and switch places with the student so she can begin the next round. Playing with three to four people, students of any age generally do not understand what is going on. After a few rounds, ask the student volunteers to leave the room while you discuss the game with the rest of the class. When the volunteers leave, tell the other students that when it is a player's turn, he or she must say where his or her hands are. Once the class understands the game, invite the student volunteers back into the classroom.

This game can last for nearly half an hour if you ask students not to reveal the secret as other students struggle. Students will announce they are "one up, one down" and you will say, "No way." It frustrates them beyond belief until you start to become very obvious with your actions. I'll say I'm "two up" and raise both arms in the air on one turn, and then I will announce that I am "two down" another time as I drop my arms to the floor. The key to the game is that what you say has to correspond to where your hands are at that moment.

This is a basic and very funny game with a very important point. The game is easy to play—once you understand the rule. Trying to figure out the rule is the hard part. This game has probably the easiest premise possible: where are your hands? However, if you do not understand the basic premise, it can be tough, frustrating, and demeaning. After the game, I ask the student volunteers how they felt during the game, and they share their frustrations and embarrassment. I then ask them if any of their classmates helped them out, and they usually say "no." I look at the class and say that I never told them that they could not help out the volunteers, but the moment the volunteers left the classroom and I shared the essence of the game, they kept that information to themselves.

Welcome to many students' daily experiences in school. I use this game to teach students to have empathy for one another and help others understand different points of view. The game is torture when it is being played, but the debriefing shows students how important it is to help one another and feel empathy for classmates who may not understand a concept that seems obvious to them.

3. What Happened?

Read any story and rewrite the ending. If you really like a story's ending, write a sequel. This game encourages students to consider alternative points of view and solutions.

4. Excuses, Excuses

Ask students to write down as many excuses as they can think of and determine how to overcome these obstacles. For example, one popular excuse for not turning in homework is "My dog ate my homework." If that were the case, how could you prevent that from happening? Students will list solutions that vary from "keep your homework away from your dog" to "feed your dog better," or "shoot your dog" (especially popular with some of my boys).

5. Problem Solver

Give students everyday problem scenarios to think about. For example, ask students for 20 possible ways to come up with the number 12. Some students will create addition and subtraction problems, some will write the number on a piece of paper and "come up" to the front of the classroom with it, and others will suggest buying a dozen eggs.

6. Find the Pattern

Allow students to determine patterns in writing, numbers, etc. For example, you could write "1, 4, 9, 16, 25, 36, 49" on the board and ask students to give the next number and their rationale (one possible answer: 64, because the numbers are consecutive perfect squares), or you could show them "fireworks, jack-o'-lanterns, turkey, presents, shamrocks" and ask for the next item in the pattern and their rationale (one possible answer: Easter eggs, because the items are related to holidays).

7. Metacognition

Encourage students to think about where and when they get their best ideas. Some people are early birds, while others are night owls. If students realize they are night owls, they need to understand that they work most effectively later in the day. I also like to brainstorm with students where they get their best ideas (e.g., in the car, in bed, in the shower) and encourage them to visit those places when they are stuck on problems. I get a lot of my best ideas in the shower, so I always had a shower curtain in my classroom. I would step behind it from time to time in front of my students to demonstrate that the shower is a place where I think more clearly. Eventually, many of my students would go behind the shower curtain to think better, too. Talking about strategies, I have found, is one of the most helpful lessons teachers can impart to students.

At the beginning or end of a lesson, I will pose different problems to students and ask them to discuss with partners or in small groups the different strategies they could use to solve the problem. We will brainstorm a list of strategies and see which small group can think of the most different effective strategies to solve any given problem.

8. The Pressure Is On

Ever play on a basketball team? When did your team shoot free throws at practice? Good coaches always have their players shoot free throws at the end of practice when the players are exhausted because most free throws are shot at the end of basketball games. Teachers need to prepare students to deal with worst-case scenarios. I want students to simulate exercises so that if they occur, they know what to do. It's the same thinking behind fire drills.

As an example for the classroom, sometimes I will ask one of my most active boys to play the role of the "Distractor" and try to break students' concentration as they try to solve problems. The Distractor can do anything he wants to break a classmate's concentration, but he cannot touch the student or shout in the student's ear.

9. Uncommon Commonality

What do polar opposites have in common? Find similarities

in differences. This is a classification game where I will divide students into two groups, one student at a time. The object of the game is for a student to figure out how I am classifying people (e.g., boys/girls, short sleeves/long sleeves, etc.). When a student guesses correctly, that student gets to swap places with the teacher and classify people.

10. What If?

Asking "What if?" is a powerful way to get students to imagine possibilities beyond rote memorization. This activity involves two components: a question and an answer.

Ask "What if?" and finish the question with an out-of-the-ordinary idea. Then have students list as many possible answers to the question as they can think of.

For example, you ask students, "What if snot was worth lots of money?"

Students try and come up with possible answers, including:

"Kindergarteners would be forced to work!"

"People would try to catch colds."

"The Federal Reserve chairman would ask citizens to blow their noses during economic crises."

11. Story Builders

Encourage students to think creatively by playing improvisational games. You need at least three players for this game, and the object is to create a silly story together. Players simply have to remember that when it is their turn, they have to do three things: take it, make it their own, and pass it along. Each player begins his or her part of the story by repeating the last thing the previous player said. Then the player adds a new action to the story. Finally, the player tacks on a third action before passing the story to the next player. Make sure players move around and mimic all actions as they dictate their stories.

For example, a student may begin by saying, "I was walking down the street, and I found a quarter, so I put it in my pocket." The next player would begin with the previous player's final thought by saying, "So I put it in my pocket, and I felt something sticky, and I pulled out some old bubble gum." The fun part about this game (especially with younger students) is that the story does not have to make sense. The player is simply responsible for three actions, and I have had children say, "I picked up a coin, and I threw it at a bird, and I drove a spaceship!"

Like all games, it may sound silly, but we are covering numerous teaching objectives and having fun in the process.

For Reflection

How do you incorporate games into your routine? Reflect on the connection raised between games and creativity. Think of a game you learned in this chapter that you will use in your classroom.

Chapter 13

Tests Are Lame

Of all the things I have learned as a teacher, one of the most important is that tests are lame. But we love tests in this country. It's all part of the "No Child Left Untested" program. Pretty soon they are going to figure out ways to test students in the womb. Ironically, a lot of the people who are so enamored with these standardized tests could have never passed them when they were students.

Is it possible to assess without tests? Think of your own strengths and weaknesses, whether they are academic, physical, or emotional. Can you think of ways to assess your abilities and comfort levels without administering a standardized test? Policymakers love tests. The amount of time, care, and attention that goes into designing tests is enormous. Tests are not exactly the best measure of students' abilities, but they certainly are a lot easier than individualizing the educational programs of every student. And don't get me wrong. I am not completely against standardized testing. I'll tell you why: They provide some useful information about a student, and some students do very well on standardized tests. But I believe we need to offer all students ways to succeed.

All this emphasis on standardized testing just reminds me of the old man's one regret. This gentleman was on his deathbed, surrounded by family and friends. He was the pride of his community: a beloved father and husband, successful businessman, and active member of his church. The man's youngest grandson approached him.

"Do you have any regrets, Grandpa?" the young boy asked.

The man summoned all his remaining strength to answer, "One... one regret." And with his dying breath, he gasped, "I wish I had scored higher on that standardized reading exam in elementary school."

Seriously, though, we are stressing students out by subjecting them to all these forms of standardized nonsense. Worse, too many teachers are leaving the profession because they feel that the emphasis is on preparing students for tests rather than actually teaching. And the sad thing is that these tests just aren't that important.

Standardized tests are here to stay, however, so I look for ways to relax my students before we partake in the dreaded four-letter word. Whenever my students and I get ready for a test, we like to sing first. Are you ready to sing?

One of the benefits of attending my workshops is that you get to experience all the movements we learn to remember the songs. My students and I love to write songs, and we usually write songs based on nursery rhymes, TV commercial jingles, TV theme songs, and Disney movies. One of the most popular songs I wrote for my students is to the beat of the song "Be Our Guest" from Disney's *Beauty and the Beast*. My version is called "Take Our Test!" and here are the lyrics (with gestures in parentheses):

"Take Our Test!"

Take our test! Take our test! (Wave arms back and forth.)

Put your name above the rest. (Raise right hand.)

To the right, you write the date there. (Move raised right hand to the right.)

Who would ask for any less? (Shrug shoulders with hands to sides, palms up,)

Use a pencil—make it sharp. You are now ready to start. (Act like you are holding a pencil and tap the top. Bring arms forward.)

Read directions very slowly—one by one, part by part. (Act like you are reading with your right index finger, thrust your arms to the right as if you were talking to somebody, and then do the same thing to the left.)

> You'll do great! You'll impress! (Put right index finger in the air! Put left index finger in the air!)
>
> You are heads above the rest. (Raise chin with right index finger.)
>
> And remember, you're the student who's the best. (Get down on one knee with arms in the air doing your best Al Jolson impersonation.)
>
> You're the smartest one. (Stand up and raise your right index finger in the air.)
>
> Now come and have some fun. (Raise left index finger in the air.)
>
> Take our test! (Dance a dance of joy in place.)
>
> Take our test! (More!)
>
> Take our test! (Big finale!)

I have learned in all my years of teaching that test scores are not the things that will stick with students. All that really matters is how you make your students feel through the things you say and do. Ten years from now, you're not going to have students return to your classroom and say, "Hi, Mr. Brassell. I remember you. You're the one who boosted me up to the next quartile." Students remember you because the day they lost their favorite soldier, you looked all over the room with them to find it. Every time their parents were late to pick them up, you were the one who waited with them. It's the little things that teachers do every day, the things that are not reflected in a test score, that truly make a difference.

Assessing Without Tests

It is possible to assess without testing. I learned that when I was in middle school.

Will Hobbs was my seventh grade reading teacher. Yup, the same Will Hobbs who went on to write such critically acclaimed books as *Bearstone* (1989), *Downriver* (1995), *Far North* (1997), the Edgar Allen Poe Award-winning *Ghost Canoe* (1998), and *Crossing the Wire* (2006)—books that sell millions of copies around the world. He used to teach reading at Miller Junior High School in the little ski-resort town of Durango, Colorado. He is one of the kindest, most inspirational mentors I have ever had. Soft-spoken Mr. Hobbs managed to achieve what no one else could: he got me to read books.

Growing up, I was never much of a reader. I earned good grades, but I absolutely detested reading. My father was a librarian, and any time I thought about libraries, I conjured up images of musty encyclopedias, uncomfortable furniture, and old ladies constantly insisting that I lower my voice. To me, a trip to the library was about as desirable as visiting the dentist.

Perhaps my lack of interest in reading was my way of rebelling against my father. Eager to flaunt my individuality, I preferred talking about my latest football game or the last movie I watched. While my parents expressed concern and would offer to buy me books and gadgets like clip-on reading lights, they opted not to force me to read anything, out of fear that it would become a chore. Despite their efforts, I picked up books only when assigned a dreaded book report in my English classes. Even then, I usually watched movie versions of the books and scanned the CliffsNotes for major plot points.

In his own laid-back fashion, Mr. Hobbs managed to change all that by creating a classroom filled with great books and great discussions about books. He convinced me to choose books that I would have never read otherwise. His indirect approach serves as the model that I train teachers of all students to use today. Mr. Hobbs got students to read by talking about books, providing lots of interesting books in his classroom, and letting students read while he read books on his own. It sounds simple, but it is still the most effective approach that I know.

Mr. Hobbs had between 20 and 30 students in each of his six class periods. Every class period was structured the same. We would find our seats, and Mr. Hobbs would tell us a little bit about what he was reading or read aloud a short passage. Then he would ask volunteers to talk about what they were reading and what they liked or disliked about certain stories and authors. This never took more than five to 10 minutes of class time, and it served as a great way to promote good books. After that, Mr. Hobbs would ask us to take out our books, or select one from his huge classroom collection, and read. He would read while we read.

When we finished a book, we would walk up to his desk and sit beside him as he asked us a few questions about the book. Once he was satisfied that we had read a book, he would give us a point. To earn an A in his class, students had to earn 20 points. Mr. Hobbs would give us a point for every 100-page book we read, and he would give us an extra point for every extra 100 pages a book contained. Mr. Hobbs also wrote the names and point totals of the top five readers of each period on the board for each class to see.

Being the competitive person I am, I wanted my name on that chalkboard. It did not matter that my interest in reading did not extend much further than *Sports Illustrated*.

By the end of the first week of the semester, five students' names were on the board for my period, and mine was not among them. That neither scared nor surprised me. I just needed a little time to find my rhythm. Lonnie Smith, however, had already earned five points, and I was dumbfounded. "What's up with her?" I asked a buddy. "She must live on a farm without electricity or something."

I was only halfway through John Steinbeck's *The Pearl* (1947), and I was already bored. Mrs. Moody had assigned the book for my English class, and I figured that I might as well read it and get credit in both classes (sort of a two-for-one deal). Mr. Hobbs knew it was required reading for my other class, but he did not lecture me when I handed it to him for my first oral book report the following week. After asking me a few questions, he caught me off guard by asking whether I had enjoyed the book.

"Not really," I replied. "I thought it was a waste of time."

He smiled and suggested I try something by S. E. Hinton.

I grabbed a copy of *Tex* (1979) because the movie was going to be on TV that month, and I read the book within a couple days. To my surprise, the book and movie were both good, and I thanked Mr. Hobbs for the recommendation. Within the next two weeks, I had devoured *The Outsiders* (1967) and *Rumble Fish* (1975), and my name was on the board in the number 5 spot by the end of the month. For the first time as a teenager, I was reading complete texts, and I even managed to enjoy them.

Then I got greedy.

Jules Verne wrote a wonderful book called *20,000 Leagues Under the Sea* (1870). The copy that Mr. Hobbs had in our classroom was over 400 pages long, making it a four-point book. Four points would boost me up to second on the top readers list, and I would be well on my way to earning my A. Let me argue in my defense that I began reading the book but found its technical passages to be longwinded and tedious. Around that same time, the Disney Channel featured the movie version of the book starring James Mason and Kirk Douglas, so I confidently walked up to Mr. Hobbs with the book in hand and movie in mind. After a few questions, I learned a valuable lesson: movie versions of books do not always coincide with the original book versions. Mr. Hobbs asked me some questions about Captain Nemo and the *Nautilus*, and it soon became apparent that I had not read the book.

Mr. Hobbs gave me the four points anyway.

I felt as small as the mayor of Lilliput, and for the rest of the semester, I read every single word of every book I brought up to Mr. Hobbs. I discovered that reading did not have to mean studying for a book report. Reading became enjoyable. Based on our classroom discussions, I selected titles that I recommend to this day, like *Call It Courage* (Sperry 1940), *Island of the Blue Dolphins* (O'Dell 1960), and my favorite, *Around the World in Eighty Days* (Verne 1873).

On one occasion, Mr. Hobbs scanned through pages of *The*

Twenty-One Balloons (Pene du Bois 1947) and for his first question, jokingly asked me how big the island was in the book. When I gave him the correct answer, he closed the book and grinned. "Yup," he said. "There's no doubt that you read this book."

By the end of the semester, I had read nearly 20 books and earned more than twice as many points as I needed for my A. I wound up finishing second in all his classes behind Lonnie Smith, who earned an astronomical 85 points. To this day, I argue that she must not have had electricity in her home, still in awe of how much she read.

In Patricia Polacco's *Thank You, Mr. Falker* (1998), a little girl has trouble with reading until her new teacher, Mr. Falker, recognizes her stuggles and spends time helping her learn to read. Mr. Hobbs was my Mr. Falker. While I could read, I had always chosen not to read. That all changed in Mr. Hobbs's class. He was the first teacher to show me that reading could be fun.

He did not motivate us with grand speeches like my drama teacher or belittling tirades like my football coach. In his gentle, soft-spoken manner, Mr. Hobbs simply asked us to choose for ourselves what we wanted to read. It sounds silly, but most adults do not empower students with such responsibility. Mr. Hobbs did not judge our choices, but rather encouraged us all to find books that inspired our passions.

Before he was writing books, Will Hobbs was a great teacher. I still recall the day in seventh grade when I told him that I wanted to write spy novels like Ian Fleming. He sat down with me after school and patiently listened to my dreadful story ideas. He had no criticisms, only suggestions. He constantly reminded me to consider the audience and to read lots of books in the same genre. He said that the one thing all great writers have in common is that they are all voracious readers.

I would be lying if I said I became a reader after that. Unfortunately, the rest of my teachers were not like Mr. Hobbs. For the rest of junior high and high school, teachers required me to read books and write book reports. I reverted back to my original state as a reluctant reader. In fact, it wasn't until I earned my doctorate that I grinned at the realization that I could finally select the books that I wanted to read. When I became a teacher, I assumed the role of Mr. Hobbs and dedicated myself to making reading enjoyable for my students. My website now provides reluctant readers of all ages with cool, short book recommendations each month: **www.lazyreaders.com**.

For this reluctant reader in seventh grade, Will Hobbs made reading a pleasurable activity rather than a drilled skill. He did it by finding a way to assess his students as readers without testing them. Today, his books inspire countless students to read for fun. For me, he will always stand out as one of the teachers who made a significant difference in my life.

For Reflection

Do you share the opinion that tests are lame? Why or why not? What ways have you used to assess students without testing? Have they been successful?

Conclusion

I take teaching very seriously.

Good teachers provide the soil that produces beautiful children who grow to become decent, responsible adults. With even the slightest bit of encouragement, a teacher can inspire the next great aviator, architect, or artist. Good teachers make sure they have a kind word for every student, every day…because they know that they may be the only person to offer that support.

Too often, good teachers are taken for granted. Has anyone ever thanked you for choosing to teach?

I mean it. Has anyone ever looked you in the eye, shook your hand, and told you "thanks"? Has anyone ever given you a great big bear hug and thanked you for teaching their child?

I spoke at a conference a few years ago and ended my speech by thanking all of the teachers in the audience for choosing to teach. A few minutes later an older woman approached me with tears in her eyes, thanking me.

"Why on earth are you thanking me?" I asked. "You're still in the classroom. You're the one who needs to be thanked."

"I've been teaching for over 30 years," she said. "And nobody has ever thanked me."

That is criminal. Municipalities should be planning parades in your honor. Good teachers should be invited regularly to the White House, featured on the covers of business magazines, and showcased at awards ceremonies. The president, the Fortune 500 executive, and the revered actor all have something in common: growing up, they all had a teacher—probably several—who believed in them.

Chances are, that class clown who now hosts a late night talk show has a teacher to thank. You were the one who laughed at his corny knock-knock jokes and told him how gifted he was.

That shy little girl who grew up to become a circuit judge has a teacher to thank. You were the one who told her how beautiful she was in front of the entire class one glorious April day.

What about that boy who always picked his scabs in class and grew up to be a surgeon? You were the one who introduced him to proper first aid.

You never know how you will influence a child. Something trivial you say today can change a child's life forever. To paraphrase the Talmud—to save one life is to save the world.

Here's a mantra that I'd like you to remember:

I make a difference
Everyday.
I change the world
In my own way.
I teach children,
And they teach me.
I am their teacher
And proud to be.

And don't forget what Michelangelo said:

"The greater danger for most of us is not that our aim is too high and we miss it, but that it is too low and we reach it."

Your students are going to achieve precisely what you believe they will achieve, so set your goals high and let your students dazzle you as they reach for the stars. Remember: You make a difference every day. Thank you for all that you do.

References Cited

Andretti, M. Quote retrieved from Quote DB on January 30, 2009. http://quotedb.com/quotes/102

Ayan, J. 1996. *Aha! 10 ways to free your creative spirit and find your great ideas.* New York: Three Rivers Press.

Coleridge, S. T. 2008. Quote retrieved from Answers.com on January 28, 2009. Samuel Taylor Coleridge…quotes by. http://www.answers.com/topic/samuel-taylor-coleridge

Dale, E. 1969. *Audio-visual methods in teaching.* 3rd ed. New York: Dryden.

Dyer, W. 2004. *The power of intention.* Carlsbad, CA: Hay House.

———. 2009. *Change your thoughts, change your life: Living the wisdom of the Tao.* Carlsbad, CA: Hay House.

Ford, H. Quote retrieved from Quotes.net on January 30, 2009. http://quotes.net/quote/6033

Fulghum, R. 1989. *All I really need to know I learned in kindergarten.* New York: Ballantine Publishing Group.

Harrell, K. 2003. *The attitude of leadership: Taking the lead and keeping it*, 103. New York: Wiley.

Holtz, L. Quote retrieved from http://quotationsbook.com/author/3529/ on January 29, 2009.

MacKenzie, G. 1998. *Orbiting the giant hairball: A corporate fool's guide to surviving with grace.* New York: Viking.

Michelangelo. Quote retrieved from http://gosmelltheflowers.com/archives/2795 on January 29, 2009.

Montessori, M. Quotes retrieved from Casa di Mir Montessori School on January 30, 2009. http://www.casadimir.org/quotes.htm

Rosenfeld, A. The benefits of board games. Retrieved from Scholastic online on January 30, 2009. http://www2.scholastic.com/browse/article.jsp?id=2060

Rylant, C. 1993. When I was young in the mountains (poem) in *When I was young in the mountains*. New York: Puffin.

Truman, H. S. Quote retrieved from Brainy Quote on January 30, 2009. http://www.brainyquote.com/quotes/authors/h/harry_s_truman.html

Ziglar, Z. 2004. *How to get what you want*. Compact disc. Simon & Schuster Audio.

TUALATIN PUBLIC LIBRARY
18878 SW MARTINAZZI AVE.
TUALATIN, OR 97062
MEMBER OF WASHINGTON COUNTY
COOPERATIVE LIBRARY SERVICES